Lula
& HER AMIGURUMI FRIENDS

A QUIRKY CLUB OF
CROCHET CHARACTERS

METEOOR BOOKS

Lula & her Amigurumi Friends
A Quirky Club of Crochet Characters
Dasha & Kate (Granny's Crochet Hook), Nour Abdallah

Use #lulaandfriends to share on Instagram.

First published July 2022
Meteoor Books, Antwerp, Belgium
www.meteoorbooks.com
hello@meteoorbooks.com

Text and images: Dasha & Kate (Granny's Crochet Hook)
Illustrations: Nour Abdallah (Nourillu)
Printed and bound by Grafistar

ISBN 978-949164-342-2
D/2022/13.531/2

A catalogue record for this book is available from the Royal
Library of Belgium.

— **Dasha & Kate (Granny's Crochet Hook)** are sisters from
St. Petersburg who share an Instagram amigurumi account and
a big love for crochet. Instagram is also the place where they first
saw Nour's character Lula and asked her if they could use her
drawing as inspiration to design a doll and pattern. And that's how
they got the ball rolling. @grannyscrochethook

....

— **Nour Abdallah** is a Berlin-based illustrator and designer who
loves toys and refuses to grow up. Having her children look at her
work and enjoy the visuals is what motivates her most! She met
Granny's Crochet Hook and they naturally started working together,
with Nour dreaming up and drawing all of the characters that
Granny's Crochet Hook turns into dolls. @nourillu

Hi from Dasha and Kate

We've been working on patterns for this book for over a year, having our ups and downs, and we're relieved to finish a little bit ahead of schedule. But now that we're asked to write an introduction, we got struck by a block. Every crochet designer whose book we're lucky to own has a beautiful background story whereas ours is not very romantic.

Growing up in post-Soviet times, we didn't have much, and this was the reason for many people to get crafty and inventive: sew beautiful dresses they couldn't afford, knit sweaters they didn't get a chance to buy, crochet doilies to decorate their homes, cross-stitch cool prints on T-shirts to impress schoolmates... But we actually were pretty happy with the clothes that had been handed down and absolutely disliked the classic lace collars we had to crochet in housekeeping classes at school. Let's blame it on Axl Rose: we never saw him wearing a granny square cardigan! In the '90s everything changed quite quickly and instead of "I have nothing to choose from", we faced the "I don't know what to choose" situation.

A few years ago we came across photos of the Hen Sisters (designed by Maria Sommer) on the Internet. After some googling we found out that all we had to do to get them was to buy a pattern, so we did. And then there was a brood of hens and "animal friends of Pica Pau" and a lot of other friends that didn't fit in a big plastic container anymore. We sold them all (without regrets) at a local market where a nice French gentleman said that what we did was very rock'n'roll. Coming from a technical background and having quite boring jobs, we didn't get to hear praise like that often, so it was the best compliment on a job we'd ever done. Crocheting quickly became one of our favorite hobbies because we can relax and meditate while making something and have a good laugh at the result. The entertaining factor is even more important for us than the therapeutic one, because having fun is our favorite ever thing to do.

This book is our first experience in making patterns on such a big scale (please go easy on us!).

Having a professional illustrator as a teammate is a major responsibility and a hell of a challenge; luckily, Nour is a crocheter herself, so she created her characters with a profound understanding of the technique and its limitations. And who would have thought we'd get to make moustached balding gentlemen and purple-haired skating grandmas! We very much hope you'll see we treated them with all due respect. We swear by Zakk Wylde's beard, we tried our best!

Let's not waste any more time chatting, let's get some coffee and get crafty because everyone needs Lula in their life and Lula's couldn't miss her little brother who, in turn, will have to have Dad to dip the pacifier in his cup, and Dad... well, you already guessed :)

Hi from Nour

As I was born in the UAE in a Lebanese family, studied in Italy and am now living and working as a designer and illustrator in Germany, I don't really like to label myself with a specific identity or culture. It has been essential to me to raise my children with an open mindset that will allow them to adapt and accept others just as they are, no matter their background.

I had a hard time finding children's books that featured a person of color as a protagonist, so I came up with a Mediterranean girl named Lula. I knew I wanted to make a children's book series about her adventures while living in a cosmopolitan city with her family, neighbors and acquaintances (who all have their own stories, beliefs and cultural backgrounds and live together peacefully). I envisioned her encounters would be playful and fun and her adventures would always carry a moral theme.

I posted the first sketch I made of Lula on my Instagram account in 2020. Dasha and Kate from Granny's Crochet Hook surprised me by reaching out and asking whether they could turn Lula and her little teddy into a crochet doll. That's how we came up with the ideas that would ultimately lead to this marvelous book. Fun fact: most of the characters in this book are inspired by real people!

I hope you'll enjoy making Lula and the rest of the crew!

HOW WE MADE THE DOLLS

The dolls in this book come in all shapes, sizes and colors, but in fact they're very close relatives technically. All the toys have similar and repetitive elements, so if you're desperately looking for a photograph of a body part and you're not seeing it, make sure to flip through the pages to find it in one of the previous patterns.

	FEET	JOINING LEGS	HEAD	HAIR	PANTS	SHIRT
DAD						
MOM						
LULA						
BO						
OPA						
OMA						
GARY						
MAJA						
HADI						
MARTHA						
TOBI						
STEFAN						
HABIBA						

* same color = similar pattern

BASIC MATERIALS

Colorful yarn

For every pattern in this book we've listed the materials used to create that design, including the yarn thickness. We've worked the samples in this book with fingering weight yarn. We've experimented with quite a few different types of yarn making these dolls, but, in our opinion, cotton and mixed (cotton/acrylic) yarns work best for these projects. As Nour's characters are colorful, but not vivid, we've chosen yarn with a rich palette.

Don't feel tied to the choice of yarn: any weight of cotton, acrylic or wool can be used as a substitute, provided you use the right crochet hook accordingly (see table on page 6 for advice).

The patterns don't give the yarn quantity. The amounts are rather small and will vary according to how loosely or tightly you crochet. You could use some of the remnants from other projects or start with a new ball of yarn. One ball of a color is usually enough.

Crochet hooks

Not only yarn, but hooks as well come in different sorts and sizes. Bigger hooks make bigger stitches than smaller ones. It's important to match the right hook size with the right weight of yarn. The crochet fabric should be quite tight, without any gaps through which the stuffing can escape. Using a smaller hook makes it easier to achieve this. Hooks are usually made from aluminum or steel. Metal hooks tend to slip between the stitches more easily. Preferably choose a crochet hook with a rubber or ergonomic handle.

You'll see that we use a small hook size for the dolls in this book. Please don't feel tied to this choice. If you prefer working with a different size, or you have a stash of heavier weight yarn that you want to use for these projects, you can change the hook and yarn accordingly (see table on page 6 for advice).

The clothes in this book are often made with a slightly bigger crochet hook than the other parts. If you're good at controlling your yarn tension when crocheting in rounds and rows, you can use the same crochet hook for all parts. If you find it tricky to control the tension just right, it would be best to choose a (slightly) bigger crochet hook size, as indicated in each pattern, instead.

Stitch marker

A stitch marker is a small clip in metal or plastic. It's a simple tool to mark your starting point and give you the assurance that you've made the right number of stitches in each round. With your stitch marker, you always mark the last stitch of a round.

Stuffing

Stuffing is crucial. If you don't stuff your doll well, it'll look sad and wilted and it's likely it'll have cellulite before you even start sewing parts together. It's particularly true for the toys' heads. A head should be as firm as a tennis ball, with no palpable lumps and holes in it. You can use a chopstick to help you with the stuffing. If you can insert a chopstick in the hole and put it right through the head, it means it needs more stuffing. We want your crocheted friend to live long, so please be patient and generous! For the stuffing, polyester fiberfill is advised. It's inexpensive, washable and non-allergenic.

ON EXPERIMENTING WITH MATERIALS

Don't get upset if the list of materials you see in a pattern seems long. You don't need to buy a roll of crafting wire just to make two tiny hairpins for Mom, or a packet of buttons to use only two of them in Bo's shoes, or a box of stuffing if you're going to make just one doll ... There's always alternative material you can use and sometimes it's even better than the one that's suggested. We spent a year making these toys over and over again and, in our opinion, there's no better stuffing than fiberfill from the cheapest IKEA pillows and no better wire for umbrella structures than flower stem holders. Don't hesitate to use yarn you consider unfashionable for making the 'hidden' parts of the bodies (for example the parts that are covered with trousers later on). Don't discard long yarn tails, as they make pretty fine embroidery threads. Do use unconventional materials, adjust, recycle, experiment and have fun!

SEWING

Having your doll in pieces, you can play with them and sometimes fix a flaw by sewing, for example, arms that came out too short a couple of rounds lower than the pattern calls for. Closing the head and then sewing it to the body will prevent stuffing from migrating inside the toy. Sewing is probably not everyone's cup of tea, but flexibility is definitely every crafter's friend.

We use a tapestry needle to sew large parts (heads) and finish off. A sharp sewing needle is used for sewing the smaller parts and for embroidery.

We like to split the yarn tail into individual strands and use only one or two out of six strands, along with a thin needle for sewing. The stitches are less visible this way.

FACIAL FEATURES

Please note that we generally find the information on 'geolocation' of facial features rather excessive, because the overall look of the toy depends on many factors: how firmly you crochet, what shade of yarn is used, how you stuff your makes. That's why we never ever embroider the face until the toy is finished. We like to use the finished shapes as an easel and see what it asks for. We highly recommend trying out different positions for the facial features, to play around with them until you find the cutest option, instead of meticulously counting rounds and stitches. A water-soluble marker or sewing pins may come in handy to mark out the facial features first. No safety eyes are used in these projects.

YARN WEIGHT	SYMBOL	RECOMMENDED HOOK BODY	RECOMMENDED HOOK OUTFIT
FINGERING WEIGHT	1	7 steel / 1.5 mm crochet hook	4 steel / 1.75 mm crochet hook
SPORT WEIGHT	2	4 or 2 steel / 2 mm crochet hook	B-1 / 2.5 mm crochet hook
LIGHT WORSTED WEIGHT	3	B-1 / 2.5 mm crochet hook	C-2 / 3 mm crochet hook
WORSTED WEIGHT	4	E-4 / 3.5 mm crochet hook	G-6 / 4 mm crochet hook

SAFETY

Please leave out crafting wire, small buttons and beads when gifting a toy to children under the age of three. Small buttons and beads can be replaced by French knots.

SKILL LEVEL

EASY (∗) INTERMEDIATE (∗ ∗) ADVANCED (∗ ∗ ∗)
Every pattern is marked with a skill level to indicate how easy it is to make. If this is your first time making amigurumi, it's best to start with an easy pattern and work up to the intermediate and advanced ones.

PATTERN STRUCTURE

- All characters are made using classic V-shaped stitches because we find the fabric made with V's is more smooth, and increases and decreases show less.
- Unless specifically mentioned, all patterns in this book are worked in continuous spirals, not in joined rounds. Crocheting in spirals can be confusing, since there's no clear indication of where a new round begins and the previous one ends. To keep track of the rounds, you can mark the end of a round with a stitch marker or safety pin. After crocheting the next round, you should end up right above your stitch marker. Move your stitch marker at the end of each round to keep track of where you are.
- At the beginning of each line you will find 'Rnd + a number' to indicate which round you are in. If a round is repeated, you'll read 'Rnd 9 – 12', for example. You then repeat this round 4 times, crocheting the stitches in rounds 9, 10, 11 and 12.
- Although we usually crochet in rounds, occasionally it happens that we switch to rows, going back and forth instead of working in continuous spirals. When we switch to rows, it will be indicated with 'Row + a number'. You end the row with a ch 1 and turn your crochetwork to start the next. Don't count this turning chain as a stitch and skip it when working the next row (unless otherwise mentioned).
- We sometimes work in joined rounds, closing the round with a slst in the first st, followed by a ch 1. When working in joined rounds, we make the first stitch in the same stitch where we made the slst.
- At the end of each line you will find the number of stitches you should have in square brackets, for example [9]. When in doubt, take a moment to check your stitch count.
- When parts of the instructions repeat throughout the round, we place them between rounded brackets, followed by the number of times this part should be worked. We do this to shorten the pattern and make it less cluttered.

THE MOST IMPORTANT NOTE

Please remember that it's up to you whether to use each pattern as a step-by-step instruction or just as a set of tips. If you're new to crocheting amigurumi, try to make one toy according to the pattern and you'll quickly figure out your preferred ways of doing things. If you're an experienced crocheter, you might find something to laugh with here, which is a good thing too. Don't forget that a crochet pattern is not a skills test: nobody will ever count the rounds and stitches you made. A toy is beautiful when you think it's beautiful and if the time you spend making it and the effort you put into it are pleasant and bring a smile to your face. We're here to have a good time, have fun crocheting!

AMIGURUMI GALLERY

With each doll, we've included a URL and QR code that will take you to that character's dedicated online gallery. Share your finished amigurumi, find inspiration in the color and yarn choices of your fellow crocheters and enjoy the fun of crocheting. Simply follow the link or scan the QR code with your mobile phone. Phones with iOS will scan the QR code automatically in camera mode. For phones with Android you may need to install a QR Reader app first.

Scan or visit
www.amigurumi.com/3900 to share pictures and find inspiration.

BASIC STITCHES

If this is your first time making amigurumi, you might find it useful to have a tutorial at hand. With the stitches explained on the following pages you can make all of the amigurumi in this book. We suggest you practice the basic stitches before you start making one of the designs. This will help you to read the patterns and abbreviations more comfortably, without having to browse back to these pages.

STITCH TUTORIAL VIDEOS

With each stitch explanation we have included a URL and QR code that will take you to an online stitch tutorial video, showing the technique step by step to help you master it even more quickly. Simply follow the link or scan the QR code with your smartphone. Phones with iOS will scan the QR code automatically in camera mode. For phones with Android you may need to install a QR Reader app first.

Scan or visit
www.stitch.show/ch
for the video tutorial

CHAIN (abbreviation: ch)
If you're working in rows, your first row will be a series of chain stitches. Use the hook to draw the yarn through the loop (1) and pull the loop until tight (2). Wrap the yarn over the hook from back to front. Pull the hook, carrying the yarn, through the loop already on your hook (3). You have now completed one chain stitch. Repeat these steps as indicated in the pattern to create a foundation chain (4).

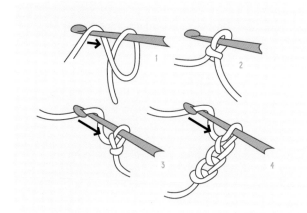

Scan or visit
www.stitch.show/sc
for the video tutorial

SINGLE CROCHET (abbreviation: sc)
Single crochet is the stitch that will be most frequently used in this book. Insert the hook into the next stitch (1) and wrap the yarn over the hook. Pull the yarn through the stitch (2). You will see that there are now two loops on the hook. Wrap the yarn over the hook again and draw it through both loops at once (3). You have now completed one single crochet (4). Insert the hook into the next stitch to continue (5).

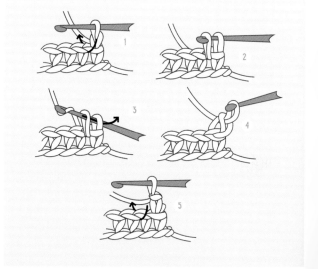

SLIP STITCH (abbreviation: slst)

A slip stitch is used to move across one or more stitches at once or to finish a piece. Insert your hook into the next stitch (1). Wrap the yarn over the hook and draw through the stitch and loop on your hook at once (2).

Scan or visit **www.stitch.show/slst** for the video tutorial

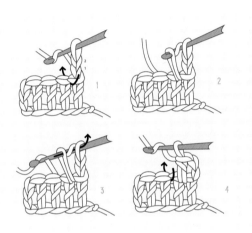

HALF DOUBLE CROCHET (abbreviation: hdc)

(When starting a new row of half double crochet, work two chain stitches to gain height.) Bring your yarn over the hook from back to front before placing the hook in the stitch (1). Wrap the yarn over the hook and draw the yarn through the stitch. You now have three loops on the hook (2). Wrap the yarn over the hook again and pull it through all three loops on the hook (3). You have completed your first half double crochet. To continue, bring your yarn over the hook and insert it in the next stitch (4).

Scan or visit **www.stitch.show/ hdc** for the video tutorial

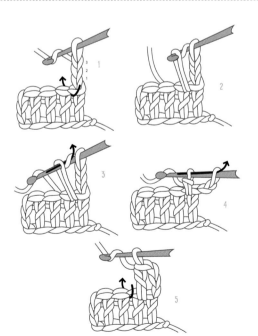

DOUBLE CROCHET (abbreviation: dc)

(When starting a new row of double crochet, work three chain stitches to gain height.) Bring your yarn over the hook from back to front before placing the hook in the stitch (1). Wrap the yarn over the hook and draw the yarn through the stitch. You now have three loops on the hook (2). Wrap the yarn over the hook again and pull it through the first two loops on the hook (3). You now have two loops on the hook. Wrap the yarn over the hook one last time and draw it through both loops on the hook (4). You have now completed one double crochet. To continue, bring your yarn over the hook and insert it in the next stitch (5).

Scan or visit **www.stitch.show/dc** for the video tutorial

TRIPLE CROCHET (abbreviation: tr)

(When starting a new row of triple crochet, work four chain stitches to gain height.) Bring your yarn over the hook twice before you insert it in the next stitch (1). Wrap the yarn over the hook and draw the yarn through the stitch (2). Wrap the yarn over the hook again and pull it through the first two loops on the hook (3). Repeat this last step twice (4, 5). You have now completed one triple crochet stitch. To continue, bring your yarn over the hook twice and insert it in the next stitch.

Scan or visit **www.stitch.show/tr** for the video tutorial

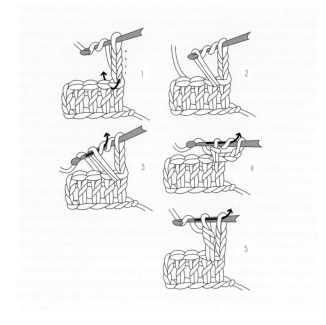

DOUBLE TRIPLE CROCHET

(abbreviation: dtr)

(When starting a new row of double triple crochet, work five chain stitches to gain height.) Bring your yarn over the hook three times and insert it in the next stitch (1). Wrap the yarn over the hook and draw the yarn through the stitch. Wrap the yarn over the hook again and pull it through the first two loops on the hook. Repeat this last step three times until you have only one leftover loop on your hook. You have now completed one double triple crochet stitch.

Scan or visit **www.stitch.show/ dtr** for the video tutorial

INCREASE (abbreviation: inc)

To increase you make two single crochet stitches in the next stitch.

Scan or visit **www.stitch.show/inc** for the video tutorial

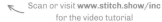

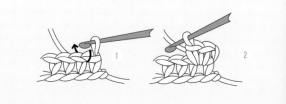

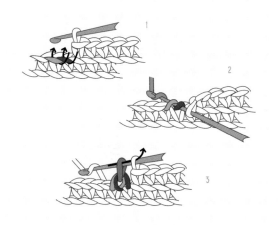

INVISIBLE DECREASE (abbreviation: dec)

The invisible decrease method will make your decrease stitch look much like the other stitches in the row, resulting in a smooth and even crochet fabric.

Insert the hook in the front loop of your first stitch. Now immediately insert your hook in the front loop of the second stitch (1). You now have three loops on your hook. Wrap the yarn over the hook and draw it through the first two loops on your hook (2). Wrap the yarn over again and draw it through the two loops remaining on your hook (3). You have now completed one invisible decrease.

Scan or visit
**www.stitch.show/
dec** for the
video tutorial

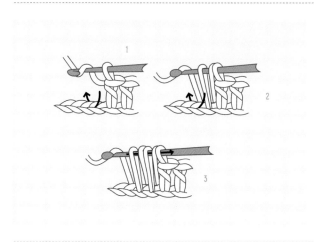

HALF DOUBLE CROCHET DECREASE
(abbreviation: hdc2tog)

Bring your yarn over the hook from back to front before placing the hook in the next stitch (1). Wrap the yarn over your hook and pull it through the stitch. You now have three loops on your hook. Repeat this from the start in the next stitch (2). You now have five loops on your hook. Wrap the yarn over your hook once more and pull it through all five loops on your hook (3). You have now decreased two half double crochet stitches.

Scan or visit
**www.stitch.show/
hdcdec** for the
video tutorial

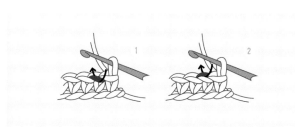

FRONT LOOPS ONLY (abbreviation: FLO)
BACK LOOPS ONLY (abbreviation: BLO)

When making a crochet stitch, you end up with two loops at the top of the stitch, a front loop towards you (1) and a back loop away from you (2). When asked to crochet FLO or BLO, you make the same stitch but leave one loop untouched.

Scan or visit
**www.stitch.show/
FLO-BLO** for the
video tutorial

MAGIC RING

A magic ring is the ideal way to start crocheting in the round. You start by crocheting over an adjustable loop and finally pull the loop tight when you have finished the required number of stitches. The advantage of this method is that there's no hole left in the center of your starting round.

Start with the yarn crossed to form a circle (1). Draw up a loop with your hook but don't pull it tight (2). Hold the circle with your index finger and thumb and wrap the working yarn over your middle finger (3). Make one chain stitch by wrapping the yarn over the hook and pulling it through the loop on your hook (4, 5). Now insert your hook into the loop and underneath the tail. Wrap the yarn over the hook and draw up a loop (6). Wrap the yarn over the hook again (7) and draw it through both loops on your hook. You have now completed your first single crochet stitch (8). Continue to crochet (repeating step 6, 7, 8) until you have the required number of stitches as mentioned in the pattern. Now grab the yarn tail and pull to draw the center of the ring tightly closed (9, 10). You can now begin your second round by crocheting into the first single crochet stitch of the magic ring. You can use a stitch marker to remember where you started.

If you don't prefer this technique, you can start each piece using the following technique: ch 2, x sc into the second chain from the hook – where x is the number of sc stitches you would make in your magic ring.

Scan or visit www.stitch.show/magicring for the video tutorial

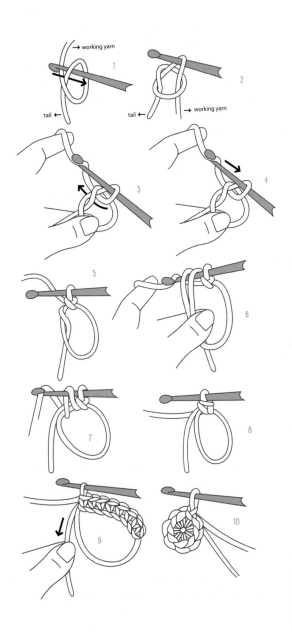

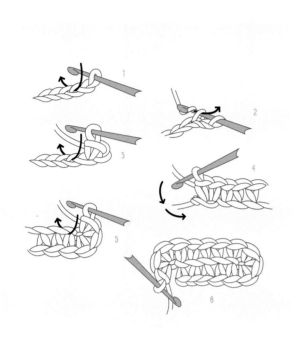

CROCHET AROUND A FOUNDATION CHAIN

Some pieces start with an oval instead of a circle. You make an oval by crocheting around a foundation chain instead of crocheting into a magic ring. Crochet a foundation chain with as many chains as mentioned in the pattern. Skip the first chain on the hook (1) and work a sc stitch in the next chain stitch (2, 3). Work your crochet stitches into each chain across as mentioned in the pattern. The last stitch before turning is usually an increase stitch (4). Now, turn your work upside down to work into the underside of the chain stitches. You'll notice that only one loop is available, simply insert your hook in this loop (5). Work your stitches into each chain across. When finished, your last stitch should be next to the first stitch you made (6). You can now continue working in spirals.

Scan or visit **www.stitch.show/oval** for the video tutorial

BACK POST OR FRONT POST
(abbreviation: BPdc, FPdc)

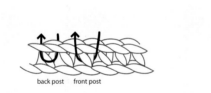

back post   front post

To make a back post or front post double crochet stitch, insert the hook from right to left around the vertical post of the next stitch according to the picture. Finish the crochet stitch as usual.

Scan or visit **www.stitch.show/BP-FP** for the video tutorial

SPIKE STITCH

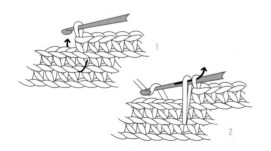

Instead of working into the two loops of the next stitch, work into the corresponding stitch in the round below (1). Wrap the yarn over the hook and draw it through the stitch. You now have two loops on your hook. Wrap the yarn over the hook once more and pull it through both loops on your hook (2). You have now completed one spike stitch.

Scan or visit **www.stitch.show/spike** for the video tutorial

Scan or visit
www.stitch.show/
picot for the
video tutorial

PICOT STITCH

Picots add a decorative touch to an edging. Make the number of chain stitches as specified in the pattern. Insert your hook in the first chain stitch you made (1), wrap the yarn around your hook and pull it through both loops on the hook. You have now completed one picot stitch (2).

BOBBLE STITCH

Bring your yarn over the hook from back to front before placing the hook in the stitch (1). Wrap the yarn over the hook and draw the yarn through the stitch. You now have three loops on the hook. Wrap the yarn over the hook again and pull it through the first two loops on the hook. One half-closed double crochet is complete, and two loops remain on the hook (2). In the same stitch, repeat the preceding steps twice. You should have four loops on your hook. Wrap the yarn over your hook and draw the yarn through all loops on the hook (3). You have now completed one 3-dc-bobble stitch. Create a bobble stitch with as many dc stitches as indicated in the pattern.

Scan or visit
www.stitch.show/
bobble for the
video tutorial

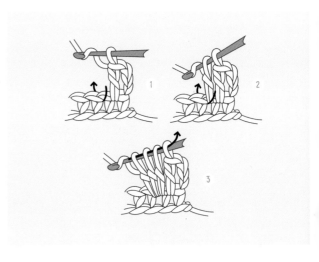

INVISIBLE COLOR CHANGE

When you want to switch from one color to the next, you work to within two stitches before a color change. Make the next stitch as usual, but don't pull the final loop through (1). Instead, wrap the new color of yarn around your hook and pull it through the remaining loops (2). To make a neat color change, you can make the first stitch in the new color a slip stitch instead of a single crochet. Don't pull the slip stitch too tight or it will be difficult to crochet into in the next round. Tie the loose tails in a knot and leave them on the inside.

Scan or visit
www.stitch.show/
colorchange
for the video tutorial

FASTENING OFF

cut the yarn a couple of inches / cm from your last stitch. Pull the yarn through the last loop until it's all the way through (1). You now have a finished knot. Thread the long tail through a yarn needle and insert your yarn needle through the back loop of the next stitch (2). This way, the finishing knot will remain invisible in your finished piece. You can use this piece of yarn to continue sewing the body pieces together.

Scan or visit **www.stitch.show/ fastenoff** for the video tutorial

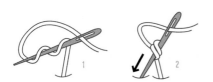

DECORATION: **FRENCH KNOT**

Insert the yarn needle from the back to the front through the stitch where you want the knot to show. Keep the tip of the needle flat against your crochetwork and wrap the yarn around your needle twice (1). Carefully pull the needle through these loops so that you end up with a double knot. Insert the needle in the crochet stitch next to the knot (2) – not in the same stitch, as this will make the knot disappear – and fasten at the back.

Scan or visit www.stitch.show/ frenchknot for the video tutorial

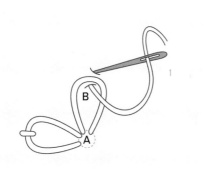

DECORATION: **LAZY DAISY STITCH**

Draw a small center circle and work from there. Insert a threaded needle from the back to the front where you want the leaf to start (A). Now insert the needle back in a stitch next to point A. Don't tighten your thread but leave a little loop. Bring your needle out at point B. Pull the thread all the way through and insert the needle in a stitch next to point B on the other side of the loop to fix the loop (1). Repeat around the center circle to create a flower.

Scan or visit www.stitch.show/ lazydaisy for the video tutorial

Scan or visit **www.stitch.show/ tapestry** for the video tutorial

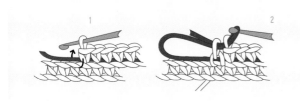

TAPESTRY CROCHET

Carry the yarn strand of one color along within the stitches (on top of the V) while continuing to crochet with the other color. Every time you make a stitch, you wrap the strand of the yarn color that you aren't using (1). Take this color on your hook in the last step of a color change (2).

DAD

Dad is a coffee shop owner who hails from the Mediterranean. Every month, he hosts a discussion forum where all neighbors can discuss topics related to the community and share their latest accomplishments.

SKILL LEVEL

*

SIZE

11.5" / 28.5 cm tall when made with the indicated yarn.

MATERIALS

- Fingering weight yarn in:
  • off-white
  • fuchsia
  • nude
  • jeans blue
  • graphite
  • brick brown (leftover)
- 7 and 4 steel / 1.5 and 1.75 mm crochet hooks
- Scraps of black, light brown and pink yarn or embroidery thread for the embroidery
- Sewing needle
- Yarn needle
- Pins
- 6 tiny buttons or beads (diameter 0.07" / 2 mm) for the shirt and trousers
- 2 flat buttons (diameter 0.8" / 2 cm) to strengthen the feet
- Stitch markers
- Fiberfill for stuffing

Scan or visit
www.amigurumi.com/3901
to share pictures and find inspiration.

Note: All parts are worked with a 7 steel / 1.5 mm crochet hook, except for the trousers (these are worked with a 4 steel / 1.75 mm crochet hook).

LEG
* make 2, start in off-white yarn

Rnd 1: start 6 sc in a magic ring [6]
Rnd 2: inc in all 6 st [12]
Rnd 3: (sc in next st, inc in next st) repeat 6 times [18]
Rnd 4: sc in next st, (inc in next st, sc in next 2 st) repeat 5 times, inc in next st, sc in next st [24]
Rnd 5: (sc in next 3 st, inc in next st) repeat 6 times [30]
Rnd 6: BLO sc in all 30 st [30]
Rnd 7 – 8: sc in all 30 st [30]
> **Note:** Insert a flat button inside the foot at this point. It's important to keep the soles flat as we want them to have the same shape as cute little hooves (picture 1).

Rnd 9: (sc in next 3 st, dec) repeat 6 times [24]
Rnd 10: sc in next st, (dec, sc in next 2 st) repeat 5 times, dec, sc in next st [18]
Change to fuchsia yarn. Stuff the leg firmly with fiberfill and continue stuffing as you go.
Rnd 11 – 18: sc in all 18 st [18]
Rnd 19: BLO sc in all 18 st [18]
Rnd 20: spike st in all 18 st [18]
Change to nude yarn.
Rnd 21: BLO sc in all 18 st [18]
Rnd 22 – 41: sc in all 18 st [18]
Change to off-white yarn.
Rnd 42: sc in all 18 st [18]
Rnd 43: spike st in all 18 st [18]
Rnd 44: BLO sc in all 18 st [18]
Rnd 45 – 50: sc in all 18 st [18]
Fasten off on the first leg and weave in the yarn end. Don't fasten off on the second leg. In the next round, we'll join both legs together and start crocheting the body.

BODY
* continue in off-white yarn

Rnd 1: ch 12 and join to the first leg with a sc (picture 2), sc in next 17 st on the first leg, sc in all 12 ch, sc in next

18 st on the second leg, sc in the opposite side of next 12 ch [60]

Crochet an additional 9 sc to move the beginning of the round to the side of the body and mark the last stitch you made. This is the new beginning of the round (picture 3).

Rnd 2: (sc in next 9 st, inc in next st) repeat 6 times [66]

Rnd 3: sc in next 5 st, (inc in next st, sc in next 10 st) repeat 5 times, inc in next st, sc in next 5 st [72]

> **Note:** You don't need military precision here because the toy is pretty big. If you miscalculated and missed a stitch or made an extra one, don't get upset, just make an increase or a decrease in the next round to reach the correct number of stitches.

Rnd 4 – 9: sc in all 72 st [72]

Rnd 10: BLO sc in all 72 st [72]

Rnd 11: spike st in all 72 st [72]

Change to jeans blue yarn.

Rnd 12: BLO sc in all 72 st [72]

Rnd 13 – 24: sc in all 72 st [72]

Rnd 25: sc in next 5 st, (dec, sc in next 10 st) repeat 5 times, dec, sc in next 5 st [66]

Rnd 26 – 29: sc in all 66 st [66]

Rnd 30: (sc in next 9 st, dec) repeat 6 times [60]

Rnd 31: sc in next 4 st, (dec, sc in next 8 st) repeat 5 times, dec, sc in next 4 st [54]

Rnd 32: (sc in next 7 st, dec) repeat 6 times [48]

Rnd 33: sc in next 3 st, (dec, sc in next 6 st) repeat 5 times, dec, sc in next 3 st [42]

Rnd 34: (sc in next 5 st, dec) repeat 6 times [36]

Rnd 35: sc in next 2 st, (dec, sc in next 4 st) repeat 5 times, dec, sc in next 2 st [30]

Fasten off, leaving a long tail for sewing. Stuff the body very firmly with fiberfill.

HEAD

✴ *in nude yarn*

Rnd 1: start 6 sc in a magic ring [6]

Rnd 2: inc in all 6 st [12]

Rnd 3: (sc in next st, inc in next st) repeat 6 times [18]

Rnd 4: sc in next st, (inc in next st, sc in next 2 st) repeat 5 times, inc in next st, sc in next st [24]

Rnd 5: (sc in next 3 st, inc in next st) repeat 6 times [30]

Rnd 6: sc in next 2 st, (inc in next st, sc in next 4 st) repeat 5 times, inc in next st, sc in next 2 st [36]

Rnd 7: (sc in next 5 st, inc in next st) repeat 6 times [42]

Rnd 8: sc in next 3 st, (inc in next st, sc in next 6 st) repeat 5 times, inc in next st, sc in next 3 st [48]

Rnd 9: (sc in next 7 st, inc in next st) repeat 6 times [54]

Rnd 10: sc in next 4 st, (inc in next st, sc in next 8 st) repeat 5 times, inc in next st, sc in next 4 st [60]

Rnd 11: (sc in next 9 st, inc in next st) repeat 6 times [66]

Rnd 12: sc in next 5 st, (inc in next st, sc in next 10 st) repeat 5 times, inc in next st, sc in next 5 st [72]

Rnd 13 – 27: sc in all 72 st [72]

Rnd 28: sc in next 5 st, (dec, sc in next 10 st) repeat 5 times, dec, sc in next 5 st [66]

Rnd 29: (sc in next 9 st, dec) repeat 6 times [60]

Rnd 30: sc in next 4 st, (dec, sc in next 8 st) repeat

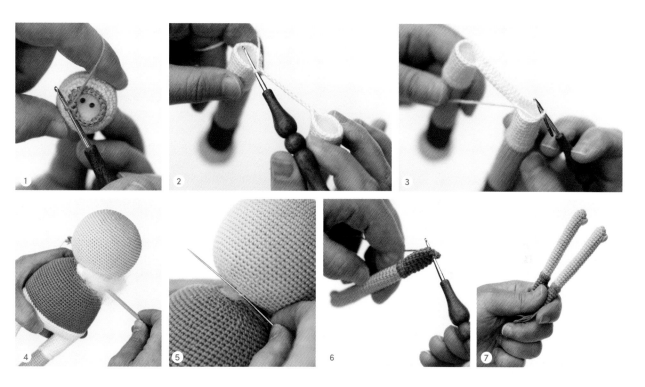

5 times, dec, sc in next 4 st [54]
Rnd 31: (sc in next 7 st, dec) repeat 6 times [48]
Stuff the head with fiberfill and continue stuffing
as you go.
Rnd 32: sc in next 3 st, (dec, sc in next 6 st) repeat
5 times, dec, sc in next 3 st [42]
Rnd 33: (sc in next 5 st, dec) repeat 6 times [36]
Rnd 34: sc in next 2 st, (dec, sc in next 4 st) repeat
5 times, dec, sc in next 2 st [30]
Rnd 35: BLO (sc in next 3 st, dec) repeat 6 times [24]
Rnd 36: sc in next st, (dec, sc in next 2 st) repeat
5 times, dec, sc in next st [18]
Finish stuffing the head very firmly.
Rnd 37: (dec, sc in next st) repeat 6 times [12]
Rnd 38: dec 6 times [6]
Fasten off, leaving a yarn tail. Using a yarn needle,
weave the yarn tail through the front loop of each
remaining stitch and pull it tight to close. Weave in the
yarn end. Sew the head and the body together using
the leftover front loops of round 34 of the head. Stuff
the neck and shoulder area with more fiberfill before
closing the seam (using a chopstick) (pictures 4-5).

ARM
* make 2, start in nude yarn

Rnd 1: start 5 sc in a magic ring [5]
Rnd 2: inc in all 5 st [10]
Rnd 3: sc in all 10 st [10]
Rnd 4: sc in next 4 st, 5-dc-bobble in next st, sc in next
5 st [10]
Rnd 5 – 24: sc in all 10 st [10]
Change to jeans blue yarn.
> **Note:** Make sure the color change is at the inside of
> the arm, add a few sc or undo a few to get to this point.
Rnd 25: BLO sc in all 10 st [10]
Rnd 26: spike st in all 10 st [10]
Rnd 27: BLO sc in all 10 st [10]
Rnd 28 – 33: sc in all 10 st [10]
Stuff only the lower half of the arm with fiberfill, so
the arms don't stick out too much after sewing. Make
a couple of additional sc or undo a few to get to the
opposite side of the thumb. Flatten the arm and work the
next round through both layers to close.

Rnd 34: sc in all 5 st [5] (pictures 6-7)
Fasten off, leaving a yarn tail for sewing. Sew the arms to the sides of the body, approximately between rounds 31 and 32.

HAIR
※ *in graphite yarn*

Rnd 1: start 6 sc in a magic ring [6]
Rnd 2: inc in all 6 st [12]
Rnd 3: (sc in next st, inc in next st) repeat 6 times [18]
Rnd 4: sc in next st, (inc in next st, sc in next 2 st) repeat 5 times, inc in next st, sc in next st [24]
Rnd 5: (sc in next 3 st, inc in next st) repeat 6 times [30]
Rnd 6: sc in next 2 st, (inc in next st, sc in next 4 st) repeat 5 times, inc in next st, sc in next 2 st [36]
Rnd 7: (sc in next 5 st, inc in next st) repeat 6 times [42]
Rnd 8: sc in next 3 st, (inc in next st, sc in next 6 st) repeat 5 times, inc in next st, sc in next 3 st [48]
Rnd 9: (sc in next 7 st, inc in next st) repeat 6 times [54]
Rnd 10: sc in next 4 st, (inc in next st, sc in next 8 st) repeat 5 times, inc in next st, sc in next 4 st [60]
Rnd 11: (sc in next 9 st, inc in next st) repeat 6 times [66]
Rnd 12: sc in next 5 st, (inc in next st, sc in next 10 st) repeat 5 times, inc in next st, sc in next 5 st [72]
Rnd 13: (sc in next 11 st, inc in next st) repeat 6 times [78]
Rnd 14 – 18: sc in all 78 st [78]
Rnd 19 – 24: hdc in next 18 st, sc in next st, slst in next st, sc in next st, hdc in next 9 st, sc in next 48 st [78]
Rnd 25: hdc in next 18 st, sc in next st, slst in next st, sc in next st, hdc in next 9 st, slst in next 2 st, ch 6, slst in second ch from hook, sc in next 3 ch, hdc in next ch, skip 1 st, sc in next 42 st, slst in next st, ch 6, slst in second ch from hook, sc in next 3 ch, hdc in next ch, skip 1 st, slst in next st [98]

> **Note:** *The worked chains will form Dad's sideburns.*

Rnd 26: slst in next st, sc in next 2 st, hdc in next 12 st, sc in next 2 st, slst in next 3 st [20] Leave the remaining stitches unworked (pictures 8-9).

Fasten off, leaving a long yarn tail for shaping the hair. The last stitch you made will be the beginning of the hair parting. Position the hair onto the head at an angle of approximately 45°. Secure it with pins. Split the yarn tail into strands and take one or two strands on a yarn needle. Mark the hair parting at the front top of the head with pins. Embroider a few short stitches through hair and head to fix the hair parting (picture 10). Weave in the yarn end. Split another yarn piece into strands and use one or two strands to sew the back side of the hair to the head. Weave in the yarn end. Pin and sew the sideburns in place. Add fiberfill under the hair to give it some volume (picture 11). Add the fiberfill in small amounts (we don't want Dad's hair to look like a mountain range). Make sure the hairdo looks smooth and even and has a nice shape. When you're happy with the way it looks, sew the front part of the hair to the forehead, using one or two strands of yarn, and weave in the yarn end.

EAR
* make 2, in nude yarn

Leave a long starting yarn tail.
Rnd 1: start 7 sc in a magic ring [7]
Pull the magic ring tightly closed and fasten off, leaving a long tail for sewing. Sew the ears to both sides of the head, right behind the sideburns. Weave in the yarn ends.

TROUSERS
* in off-white yarn, with a 4 steel / 1.75 mm crochet hook

Ch 72 and join with a slst to make a circle. Make sure the chain isn't twisted.
Rnd 1: sc in all 72 ch [72]
> **Note:** Try it on, the circle should fit the body nicely underneath the shirt hem. If it's too tight, consider using a bigger hook. If it's too loose, you might want to use a smaller hook.

Rnd 2 – 15: sc in all 72 st [72]
Flatten your work and divide it into 36 stitches for each trouser leg. Continue working the first trouser leg.
Rnd 16: sc in next 36 st, skip next 36 st [36]
Continue working on these 36 stitches only.
Rnd 17 – 41: sc in all 36 st [36]
> **Note:** Try the trousers on as you go. You may want to crochet a round or two less or more. We like them quite short, so you can see Dad's socks.

Rnd 42: slst in all 36 st [36]
Fasten off and weave in the yarn end on the wrong side of your work. Pull up a loop of off-white yarn in the next unworked stitch of round 15 of the trousers to make the second trouser leg (pictures 12-13).
Rnd 16 – 42: repeat the instructions for the first trouser leg.
Fasten off and weave in the yarn end.

BELT
* in graphite yarn, with a 4 steel / 1.75 mm crochet hook

Hold the trousers with the legs pointing towards you.
Pull up a loop of graphite yarn in a stitch of round 1 of

the trousers, preferably at the back.
Rnd 1: slst in all 72 st [72]
Rnd 2: BLO sc in all 72 st [72]
Rnd 3: spike st in all 72 st [72]
Change to off-white yarn.
Rnd 4: BLO slst in all 72 st [72] (pictures 14-15)
Fasten off and weave in the yarn end. Using scraps of off-white yarn, embroider four belt loops (pictures 16-17). You can mark the places where you want the belt loops to be with a water-soluble marker first.

SUSPENDERS
* in orange yarn

Ch 53. Crochet in rows.
Row 1: start in fourth ch from hook, slst in next 36 ch, ch 39, start in fourth ch from hook, slst in next 36 ch, sc in remaining 14 ch.
Fasten off, leaving a long tail for sewing. Sew the bottom central part of the suspenders to the center back of

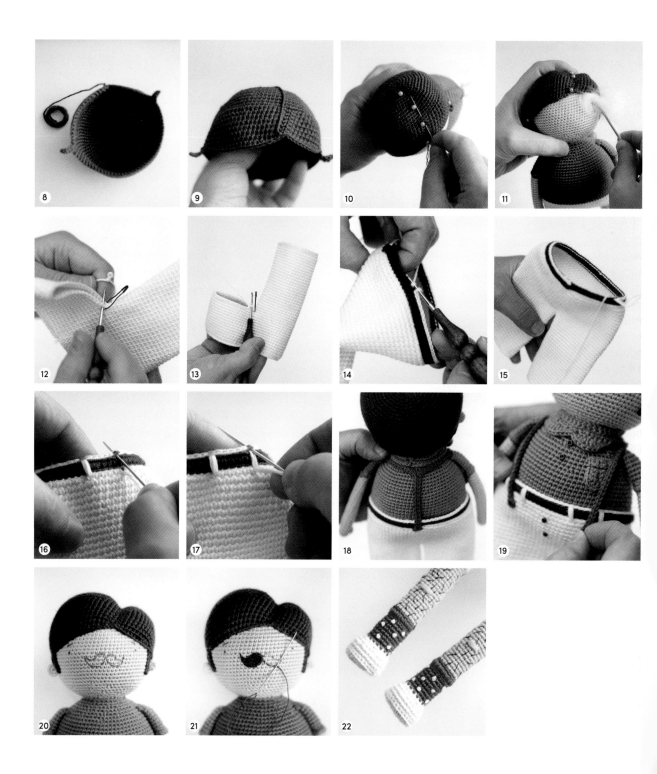

round 1 of the trousers (pictures 18). Put the trousers on, pull the suspenders over the shoulders and sew the ends to the front of the trousers. If you want to make the suspenders removable, you can sew two tiny buttons to the trousers matching the buttonholes on the suspender ends (picture 19).

COLLAR
✳ *in jeans blue yarn*

diagram 4 page 135

Ch 38. Crochet in rows.
Row 1: start in second ch from hook, sc in next 37 ch, ch 1, turn [37]
Row 2: sc in next 3 st, (inc in next st, sc in next 5 st) repeat 5 times, inc in next st, sc in next 3 st, ch 1, turn [43]
Row 3: sc in next 16 st, hdc in next st, dc in next 2 st, hdc in next st, sc in next st, slst in next st, sc in next st, hdc in next st, dc in next 2 st, hdc in next st, sc in next 16 st, ch 1, turn [43]
Row 4: slst in next 15 st, sc in next st, hdc inc in next st, dc inc in next 2 st, hdc inc in next st, sc in next st, slst in next st, sc in next st, hdc inc in next st, dc inc in next 2 st, hdc inc in next st, sc in next st, slst in next 15 st [51]
Fasten off, leaving a long tail for sewing. Sew the collar between rounds 34-35 of the body (picture 19).

BREAST POCKET
✳ *in jeans blue yarn*

diagram 1 page 135

Ch 5. Stitches are worked around both sides of the foundation chain. Crochet in rows.
Row 1: start in second ch from hook, sc in next 3 ch, 5 sc in next ch. Continue on the other side of the foundation chain, sc in next 3 ch, ch 1, turn [11]
Row 2: sc in next 4 st, inc in next 3 st, sc in next 4 st [14]
Fasten off and weave in the yarn end on the wrong side of your work. Using a single strand of jeans blue yarn, sew the pocket to the shirt.

FINISHING TOUCHES

• Embroider the facial features. A water-soluble marker or sewing pins may come in handy to mark out the position of the eyes, mouth, moustache and cheeks first. The eyes are embroidered using one or two strands of graphite yarn or black embroidery thread. Position the eyes on round 19 of the head, with an interspace of approximately 18 stitches. Embroider the eyebrows and moustache using light brown embroidery thread (pictures 20-21). Embroider the cheeks underneath the eyes using pink embroidery thread.
• Sew tiny buttons or beads (or make French knots) on the front of the trousers and the shirt.
• Make a few stitches here and there to mark out funny details (add a seam on the pocket, mimic the knees using nude yarn, add some hair to the legs using graphite yarn).
• Decorate the socks with polka dots (you can make them with French knots using white yarn) (picture 22).

MOM

Mom is mother to Lula and Bo. She works as a handbag designer and sells her unique handmade items at her boutique next to Daddy's coffee shop. She loves to drink her matcha tea in the mornings and work on knitting projects at night.

SKILL LEVEL

✳

SIZE

11.5" / 28.5 cm tall when made with the indicated yarn.

MATERIALS

- Fingering weight yarn in:
  • off-white
  • lilac
  • nude
  • graphite
- 7 and 4 steel / 1.5 and 1.75 mm crochet hooks
- Scraps of black and pink yarn or embroidery thread for the embroidery
- Sewing needle
- Yarn needle
- Pins
- 3 tiny buttons or beads (diameter 0.07"/ 2 mm) for the dress
- 4 shiny beads (diameter 0.11"/ 3 mm) for the earrings and the hairpins
- 2 flat buttons (diameter 0.6"/ 1.7 cm) to strengthen the feet
- 4" / 10 cm of florist wire for the hairpins
- Hot glue
- Stitch markers
- Fiberfill for stuffing

Scan or visit
www.amigurumi.com/3902
to share pictures and find inspiration.

Note: *All parts are worked with a 7 steel / 1.5 mm crochet hook, except for the dress (this is worked with a 4 steel / 1.75 mm crochet hook).*

LEG

✳ *make 2, start in graphite yarn*

Rnd 1: start 7 sc in a magic ring [7]
Rnd 2: inc in all 7 st [14]
Rnd 3: (sc in next st, inc in next st) repeat 7 times [21]
Rnd 4: BLO sc in all 21 st [21]
Rnd 5: sc in all 21 st [21]

> **Note:** *Insert a flat button inside the foot at this point. It's important to keep the soles flat as we want them to have the same shape as cute little hooves.*

Rnd 6: (sc in next st, dec) repeat 7 times [14]
Change to nude yarn.
Rnd 7 – 12: sc in all 14 st [14]
Stuff the leg firmly with fiberfill and continue stuffing as you go.
Rnd 13: inc in next st, sc in next 13 st [15]
Rnd 14 – 18: sc in all 15 st [15]
Rnd 19: sc in next 7 st, inc in next st, sc in next 7 st [16]
Rnd 20 – 24: sc in all 16 st [16]
Rnd 25: inc in next st, sc in next 15 st [17]
Rnd 26 – 30: sc in all 17 st [17]
Rnd 31: sc in next 8 st, inc in next st, sc in next 8 st [18]
Rnd 32 – 36: sc in all 18 st [18]
Change to off-white yarn.
Rnd 37: BLO sc in all 18 st [18]
Rnd 38: spike st in all 18 st [18]
Rnd 39: BLO inc in all 18 st [36]
Rnd 40 – 44: sc in all 36 st [36]
Fasten off on the first leg, leaving a yarn tail. Don't fasten off on the second leg. In the next round, we'll join both legs together and start crocheting the body.

BODY

✳ *continue in off-white yarn*

Rnd 1: sc in a st on the first leg to join, sc in next 32 st on the first leg, leave the remaining 3 st unworked, skip 3 st on the second leg, sc in the 4th stitch of the second leg, sc in next 32 st on the second leg [66]

Rnd 2: sc in all 66 st [66] (picture 1)

Use the yarn tail left on the first leg to sew the gap between the legs closed (pictures 2-3).

Rnd 3 – 12: sc in all 66 st [66]

Change to nude yarn.

> **Note:** You can use yarn in any color you have on hand to make the rest of the body (except for the 3-4 last rounds), as it's going to be covered with the dress anyway.

Rnd 13: sc in all 66 st [66]

Rnd 14: (sc in next 9 st, dec) repeat 6 times [60]

Rnd 15 – 19: sc in all 60 st [60]

Rnd 20: sc in next 4 st, (dec, sc in next 8 st) repeat 5 times, dec, sc in next 4 st [54]

Rnd 21 – 25: sc in all 54 st [54]

Rnd 26: (sc in next 7 st, dec) repeat 6 times [48]

Rnd 27: sc in all 48 st [48]

Rnd 28: sc in next 3 st, (dec, sc in next 6 st) repeat 5 times, dec, sc in next 3 st [42]

Rnd 29: sc in all 42 st [42]

Rnd 30: (sc in next 5 st, dec) repeat 6 times [36]

Rnd 31: sc in all 36 st [36]

Rnd 32: sc in next 2 st, (dec, sc in next 4 st) repeat 5 times, dec, sc in next 2 st [30]

Rnd 33: sc in all 30 st [30]

Fasten off, leaving a long tail for sewing. Stuff the body very firmly with fiberfill.

ARM

* make 2, in nude yarn

Rnd 1: start 5 sc in a magic ring [5]

Rnd 2: inc in all 5 st [10]

Rnd 3: sc in all 10 st [10]

Rnd 4: sc in next 4 st, 5-dc-bobble in next st, sc in next 5 st [10]

Rnd 5 – 31: sc in all 10 st [10]

Stuff only the lower half of the arm with fiberfill, so the arms don't stick out too much after sewing. Make a couple of additional sc or undo a few to get to the opposite side of the thumb. Flatten the arm and work the next round through both layers to close.

Rnd 32: sc in all 5 st [5]

Fasten off, leaving a yarn tail for sewing. Sew the arms to the sides of the body, approximately between rounds 27 and 28.

DRESS

* in lilac yarn, with a 4 steel / 1.75 mm crochet hook

Ch 42 and join with a slst to make a circle. Make sure the chain isn't twisted.

Rnd 1: sc in all 42 ch [42]

Rnd 2: sc in next 3 st, (inc in next st, sc in next 6 st) repeat 5 times, inc in next st, sc in next 3 st [48]

Rnd 3: sc in next 8 st, ch 11, skip next 8 st, sc in next 16 st, ch 11, skip next 8 st, sc in next 8 st [32 + 22 ch] (picture 4)

Rnd 4: sc in all 54 st [54]

Rnd 5: sc in next 4 st, (inc in next st, sc in next 8 st) repeat 5 times, inc in next st, sc in next 4 st [60]

Rnd 6: (sc in next 9 st, inc in next st) repeat 6 times [66]

Rnd 7 – 11: sc in all 66 st [66]

Rnd 12: (sc in next 21 st, inc in next st) repeat 3 times [69]

Rnd 13 – 17: sc in all 69 st [69]

Rnd 18: (sc in next 22 st, inc in next st) repeat 3 times [72]

Rnd 19 – 23: sc in all 72 st [72]

Rnd 24: (sc in next 23 st, inc in next st) repeat 3 times [75]

Rnd 25 – 29: sc in all 75 st [75]

Rnd 30: (sc in next 24 st, inc in next st) repeat 3 times [78]

Rnd 31 – 35: sc in all 78 st [78]

Rnd 36: slst in all 78 st [78]

Fasten off and weave in the yarn end.

DRESS PLACKET

* in lilac yarn, with a 4 steel / 1.75 mm crochet hook

Ch 19. Stitches are worked around both sides of the foundation chain.

Rnd 1: start in second ch from hook, sc in next 17 ch, 5 sc in next ch. Continue on the other side of the foundation chain, sc in next 17 ch [39]

Fasten off, leaving a long tail for sewing. Using a single strand of lilac yarn, sew the placket in the middle of the dress (pictures 5-6). Decorate it with 3-4 tiny buttons.

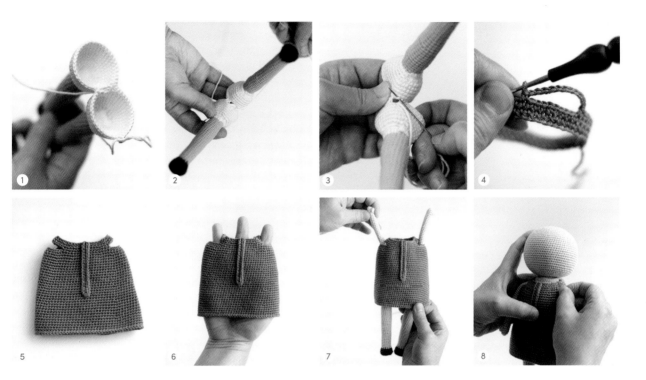

Put the dress on (picture 7).

HEAD

* in nude yarn

Rnd 1: start 6 sc in a magic ring [6]
Rnd 2: inc in all 6 st [12]
Rnd 3: (sc in next st, inc in next st) repeat 6 times [18]
Rnd 4: sc in next st, (inc in next st, sc in next 2 st) repeat 5 times, inc in next st, sc in next st [24]
Rnd 5: (sc in next 3 st, inc in next st) repeat 6 times [30]
Rnd 6: sc in next 2 st, (inc in next st, sc in next 4 st) repeat 5 times, inc in next st, sc in next 2 st [36]
Rnd 7: (sc in next 5 st, inc in next st) repeat 6 times [42]
Rnd 8: sc in next 3 st, (inc in next st, sc in next 6 st) repeat 5 times, inc in next st, sc in next 3 st [48]
Rnd 9: (sc in next 7 st, inc in next st) repeat 6 times [54]
Rnd 10: sc in next 4 st, (inc in next st, sc in next 8 st) repeat 5 times, inc in next st, sc in next 4 st [60]
Rnd 11: (sc in next 9 st, inc in next st) repeat 6 times [66]
Rnd 12: sc in next 5 st, (inc in next st, sc in next 10 st) repeat 5 times, inc in next st, sc in next 5 st [72]
Rnd 13 – 27: sc in all 72 st [72]
Rnd 28: sc in next 5 st, (dec, sc in next 10 st) repeat 5 times, dec, sc in next 5 st [66]
Rnd 29: (sc in next 9 st, dec) repeat 6 times [60]
Rnd 30: sc in next 4 st, (dec, sc in next 8 st) repeat 5 times, dec, sc in next 4 st [54]
Rnd 31: (sc in next 7 st, dec) repeat 6 times [48]
Stuff the head with fiberfill and continue stuffing as you go.
Rnd 32: sc in next 3 st, (dec, sc in next 6 st) repeat 5 times, dec, sc in next 3 st [42]
Rnd 33: (sc in next 5 st, dec) repeat 6 times [36]
Rnd 34: sc in next 2 st, (dec, sc in next 4 st) repeat 5 times, dec, sc in next 2 st [30]
Rnd 35: BLO (sc in next 3 st, dec) repeat 6 times [24]
Rnd 36: sc in next st, (dec, sc in next 2 st) repeat 5 times, dec, sc in next st [18]
Finish stuffing the head very firmly.
Rnd 37: (dec, sc in next st) repeat 6 times [12]
Rnd 38: dec 6 times [6]
Fasten off, leaving a yarn tail. Using a yarn needle,

Rnd 5: (sc in next 3 st, inc in next st) repeat 6 times [30]
Rnd 6: sc in next 2 st, (inc in next st, sc in next 4 st) repeat 5 times, inc in next st, sc in next 2 st [36]
Rnd 7: (sc in next 5 st, inc in next st) repeat 6 times [42]
Rnd 8: sc in next 3 st, (inc in next st, sc in next 6 st) repeat 5 times, inc in next st, sc in next 3 st [48]
Rnd 9: (sc in next 7 st, inc in next st) repeat 6 times [54]
Rnd 10: sc in next 4 st, (inc in next st, sc in next 8 st) repeat 5 times, inc in next st, sc in next 4 st [60]
Rnd 11: (sc in next 9 st, inc in next st) repeat 6 times [66]
Rnd 12: sc in next 5 st, (inc in next st, sc in next 10 st) repeat 5 times, inc in next st, sc in next 5 st [72]
Rnd 13: (sc in next 11 st, inc in next st) repeat 6 times [78]
Rnd 14 – 18: sc in all 78 st [78]
Rnd 19 – 24: sc in next 33 st, hdc in next 21 st, sc in next st, slst in next st, sc in next st, hdc in next 21 st [78]
Rnd 25: sc in next 37 st, hdc in next 17 st, sc in next st, slst in next st, sc in next st, hdc in next 17 st, sc in next 4 st [78]
Rnd 26: sc in next 41 st, hdc in next 13 st, sc in next st, slst in next st [56] Leave the remaining stitches un-worked.

Fasten off, leaving a long yarn tail for shaping the hair. The last stitch you made will be the beginning of the hair parting. Position the hair onto the head at an angle of approximately 45°. Secure it with pins. Split the yarn tail into strands and take one or two strands on a yarn needle. Mark the hair parting at the front top of the head with pins. Embroider a few short stitches through hair and head to fix the hair parting (see pictures in Dad's pattern, page 22). Sew the back side of the hair to the head. Add fiberfill under the hair to give it some volume. Add the fiberfill in small amounts (we don't want Mom's hair to look like a mountain range). Make sure the hairdo looks smooth and even and has a nice shape. When you're happy with the way it looks, sew the front part of the hair to the forehead, using one or two strands of yarn, and weave in the yarn end.

weave the yarn tail through the front loop of each remaining stitch and pull it tight to close. Weave in the yarn end. Sew the head and the body together using the leftover front loops of round 34 of the head (picture 8). Stuff the neck area with more fiberfill before closing the seam (using a chopstick).

HAIR
* in graphite yarn

Rnd 1: start 6 sc in a magic ring [6]
Rnd 2: inc in all 6 st [12]
Rnd 3: (sc in next st, inc in next st) repeat 6 times [18]
Rnd 4: sc in next st, (inc in next st, sc in next 2 st) repeat 5 times, inc in next st, sc in next st [24]

HAIR BUN
* in graphite yarn

Rnd 1: start 6 sc in a magic ring [6]

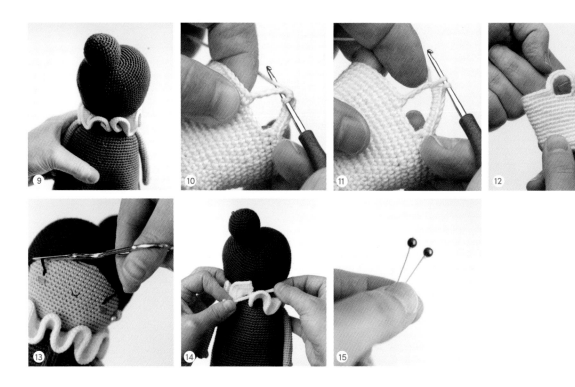

Rnd 2: inc in all 6 st [12]
Rnd 3: (sc in next st, inc in next st) repeat 6 times [18]
Rnd 4: sc in next st, (inc in next st, sc in next 2 st) repeat 5 times, inc in next st, sc in next st [24]
Rnd 5: (sc in next 3 st, inc in next st) repeat 6 times [30]
Rnd 6: sc in next 2 st, (inc in next st, sc in next 4 st) repeat 5 times, inc in next st, sc in next 2 st [36]
Rnd 7 – 11: sc in all 36 st [36]
Rnd 12: sc in next 5 st, (dec, sc in next 10 st) repeat 2 times, dec, sc in next 5 st [33]
Rnd 13: (sc in next 9 st, dec) repeat 3 times [30]
Rnd 14: sc in next 4 st, (dec, sc in next 8 st) repeat 2 times, dec, sc in next 4 st [27]
Rnd 15: (sc in next 7 st, dec) repeat 3 times [24]
Rnd 16: sc in next 3 st, (dec, sc in next 6 st) repeat 2 times, dec, sc in next 3 st [21]
Rnd 17: (sc in next 5 st, dec) repeat 3 times [18]
Slst in next st. Fasten off, leaving a long tail for sewing. Stuff the hair bun with fiberfill and sew it on top of the head, slightly skewed to one side (picture 9).

EAR
* make 2, in nude yarn

Leave a long starting yarn tail.
Rnd 1: start 5 sc in a magic ring [5]
Pull the magic ring tightly closed and fasten off, leaving a tail for sewing. Sew the ears to both sides of the head, right under the edge of the hair.

COLLAR
* in off-white yarn

Ch 19. Crochet in rows.
Row 1: start in second ch from hook, slst in next 18 ch, ch 55, start in second ch from hook, slst in next 18 ch, sc in next 36 ch, ch 2, turn [72]
From now on, work along the middle part of the collar only (36 sc stitches), as the 18 stitches on each side will form the collar ties.
Row 2: dc inc in all 36 st, ch 2, turn [72]

Row 3: dc inc in all 72 st, ch 2, turn [144]

Row 4: (dc in next st, dc inc in next st) repeat 72 times, ch 1, turn [216]

Row 5: slst in all 216 st [216]

Fasten off and weave in the yarn end.

PURSE

✳ *in off-white yarn*

Ch 11. Stitches are worked around both sides of the foundation chain.

Rnd 1: start in second ch from hook, sc in next 9 ch, 3 sc in next ch. Continue on the other side of the foundation chain, sc in next 8 ch, inc in next ch [22]

Rnd 2: inc in next st, sc in next 8 st, inc in next 3 st, sc in next 8 st, inc in next 2 st [28]

Rnd 3: BLO sc in all 28 st [28]

Rnd 4: sc in all 28 st [28]

Rnd 5: sc in next 3 st, (inc in next st, sc in next 6 st) repeat 3 times, inc in next st, sc in next 3 st [32]

Rnd 6 – 7: sc in all 32 st [32]

Rnd 8: (sc in next 7 st, inc in next st) repeat 4 times [36]

Rnd 9 – 10: sc in all 36 st [36]

Rnd 11: sc in next 4 st, (inc in next st, sc in next 8 st) repeat 3 times, inc in next st, sc in next 4 st [40]

Rnd 12 – 13: sc in all 40 st [40]

Rnd 14: sc in next 9 st, ch 10, skip 3 st, sc in next 17 st, ch 10, skip 3 st, sc in next 8 st [34 + 20 ch]

> **Note:** When working the handles in round 15, you insert the hook underneath the chain, not in the individual chain stitches, so the stitches are "wrapping" the chain, forming the handles.

Rnd 15: sc in next 9 st, make 14 sc in the ch-10-space, sc in next 17 st, make 14 sc in the ch-10-space, sc in next 7 st, slst in next st [62] (pictures 10-11)

Fasten off and weave in the yarn end (picture 12).

FINISHING TOUCHES

• Embroider the facial features. A water-soluble marker or sewing pins may come in handy to mark out the position of the eyes, mouth and cheeks first. The eyes are embroidered using one or two strands of graphite yarn or black embroidery thread. Position them on round 17 of the head, with an interspace of approximately 16 stitches. Embroider the cheeks underneath the eyes using pink embroidery thread.

• Give Mom some eyelashes by pulling pieces of black embroidery thread through the stitches (picture 13).

• Make a few stitches on each leg (5-6 rounds below the edge of the dress) using nude yarn to mimic the knees.

• Sew small beads on the ears to mimic earrings.

• Put the collar around Mom's neck and tie a knot at the back (picture 14).

• Glue a bead on top of a piece of crafting wire to make a hairpin to decorate Mom's hairdo (picture 15).

LULA

Lula is a curious and kind-hearted girl. She loves to collect chestnuts and paint them to make necklaces. She easily makes new friends and cannot stand bullies! Lula loves helping her dad at the coffee shop every once in a while, and spends her allowance on bang snaps.

SKILL LEVEL

* *

SIZE

Lula: 8" / 20.5 cm tall when made with the indicated yarn. Lula's little friend: 2.3" / 6 cm tall when made with the indicated yarn.

MATERIALS

- Fingering weight yarn in:
  • off-white
  • jeans blue
  • nude
  • graphite
  • fuchsia (leftover)
  • red (leftover)
  • brown
- 7 and 4 steel / 1.5 and 1.75 mm crochet hooks
- Scraps of black and pink yarn or embroidery thread for the embroidery
- Sewing needle
- Yarn needle
- Pins
- 4 tiny buttons or beads (diameter 1/16" / 2 mm) for the jumpsuit
- 2 flat buttons (diameter 0.8" / 2 cm) to strengthen the feet
- Stitch markers
- Fiberfill for stuffing

Scan or visit
www.amigurumi.com/3903
to share pictures and find inspiration.

Note: *All parts are worked with a 7 steel / 1.5 mm crochet hook, except for the jumpsuit (this is worked with a 4 steel / 1.75 mm crochet hook).*

LEG

* *make 2, start in graphite yarn*

Rnd 1: start 6 sc in a magic ring [6]
Rnd 2: inc in all 6 st [12]
Rnd 3: (sc in next st, inc in next st) repeat 6 times [18]
Rnd 4: sc in next st, (inc in next st, sc in next 2 st) repeat 5 times, inc in next st, sc in next st [24]
Rnd 5: BLO sc in all 24 st [24]
Rnd 6: sc in all 24 st [24]
Rnd 7: sc in next st, (dec, sc in next 2 st) repeat 5 times, dec, sc in next st [18]

> **Note:** *Insert a flat button inside the foot at this point. It's important to keep the soles flat as we want them to have the same shape as cute little hooves.*

Rnd 8: (sc in next st, dec) repeat 6 times [12]
Change to nude yarn. Stuff the leg firmly with fiberfill and continue stuffing as you go.
Rnd 9 – 16: sc in all 12 st [12]
Fasten off on the first leg, leaving a yarn tail. Don't fasten off on the second leg. In the next round, we'll join both legs together and start crocheting the body.

BODY

* *continue in nude yarn*

> **Note:** *You can use yarn in any color you have on hand for crocheting rounds 1-29 of the body, as it's going to be covered with the jumpsuit anyway.*

Rnd 1: ch 18 and join to the first leg with a sc, sc in next 11 st on the first leg, sc in next 18 ch, sc in next 12 st on the second leg, sc in the opposite side of next 18 ch [60]
Crochet an additional 6 sc to move the beginning of the round to the side of the body and mark the last stitch you made. This is the new beginning of the round.

> **Note:** *You don't need military precision here because*

the toy is pretty big. If you miscalculated and missed a stitch or made an extra one, don't get upset, just make an increase or a decrease in the next round to reach the correct number of stitches.

Rnd 2: sc in all 60 st [60]
Rnd 3: (sc in next 9 st, inc in next st) repeat 6 times [66]
Make sure the legs are stuffed very firmly at this point.
Rnd 4 – 7: sc in all 66 st [66]
Rnd 8: sc in next 5 st, (inc in next st, sc in next 10 st) repeat 5 times, inc in next st, sc in next 5 st [72]
Rnd 9 – 11: sc in all 72 st [72]
Rnd 12: (sc in next 11 st, inc in next st) repeat 6 times [78]
Rnd 13 – 22: sc in all 78 st [78]
Rnd 23: (sc in next 11 st, dec) repeat 6 times [72]
Stuff the body with fiberfill and continue stuffing as you go.
Rnd 24 – 29: sc in all 72 st [72]
Crochet a few additional sc to move the beginning of the round back to the side of the body. Change to off-white yarn and crochet the next rounds in a stripe pattern, alternating off-white and graphite yarn with each round.
Rnd 30 – 31: sc in all 72 st [72]
Rnd 32: sc in next 5 st, (dec, sc in next 10 st) repeat 5 times, dec, sc in next 5 st [66]
Rnd 33 – 36: sc in all 66 st [66]
Rnd 37: (sc in next 9 st, dec) repeat 6 times [60]
Rnd 38: sc in next 4 st, (dec, sc in next 8 st) repeat 5 times, dec, sc in next 4 st [54]
Rnd 39: (sc in next 7 st, dec) repeat 6 times [48]
Fasten off the graphite yarn. Continue with off-white yarn.
Rnd 40: sc in next 3 st, (dec, sc in next 6 st) repeat 5 times, dec, sc in next 3 st [42]
Change to nude yarn, but don't fasten off the off-white yarn just yet. Leave it hanging on the outside of your work.
Rnd 41: BLO (sc in next 5 st, dec) repeat 6 times [36]
Rnd 42: sc in next 2 st, (dec, sc in next 4 st) repeat 5 times, dec, sc in next 2 st [30]
Fasten off, leaving a long tail for sewing.

COLLAR
* in off-white yarn

Take the off-white yarn on the outside of your work on your crochet hook and start in the leftover front loop of round 40 where the off-white yarn appears.
Rnd 1: FLO sc in all 42 st [42]
Slst in next st. Fasten off and weave in the yarn end.
Stuff the body very firmly with fiberfill (picture 1).

HEAD
* in nude yarn

Rnd 1: start 6 sc in a magic ring [6]
Rnd 2: inc in all 6 st [12]
Rnd 3: (sc in next st, inc in next st) repeat 6 times [18]
Rnd 4: sc in next st, (inc in next st, sc in next 2 st) repeat 5 times, inc in next st, sc in next st [24]
Rnd 5: (sc in next 3 st, inc in next st) repeat 6 times [30]
Rnd 6: sc in next 2 st, (inc in next st, sc in next 4 st) repeat 5 times, inc in next st, sc in next 2 st [36]
Rnd 7: (sc in next 5 st, inc in next st) repeat 6 times [42]
Rnd 8: sc in next 3 st, (inc in next st, sc in next 6 st) repeat 5 times, inc in next st, sc in next 3 st [48]
Rnd 9: (sc in next 7 st, inc in next st) repeat 6 times [54]
Rnd 10: sc in next 4 st, (inc in next st, sc in next 8 st) repeat 5 times, inc in next st, sc in next 4 st [60]
Rnd 11: (sc in next 9 st, inc in next st) repeat 6 times [66]
Rnd 12 – 25: sc in all 66 st [66]
Rnd 26: (sc in next 9 st, dec) repeat 6 times [60]
Rnd 27: sc in next 4 st, (dec, sc in next 8 st) repeat 5 times, dec, sc in next 4 st [54]
Rnd 28: (sc in next 7 st, dec) repeat 6 times [48]
Stuff the head with fiberfill and continue stuffing as you go.
Rnd 29: sc in next 3 st, (dec, sc in next 6 st) repeat 5 times, dec, sc in next 3 st [42]
Rnd 30: (sc in next 5 st, dec) repeat 6 times [36]
Rnd 31: sc in next 2 st, (dec, sc in next 4 st) repeat 5 times, dec, sc in next 2 st [30]
Rnd 32: BLO (sc in next 3 st, dec) repeat 6 times [24]
Rnd 33: sc in next st, (dec, sc in next 2 st) repeat 5 times, dec, sc in next st [18]
Finish stuffing the head very firmly.
Rnd 34: (dec, sc in next st) repeat 6 times [12]
Rnd 35: dec 6 times [6]
Fasten off, leaving a yarn tail. Using a yarn needle, weave the yarn tail through the front loop of each

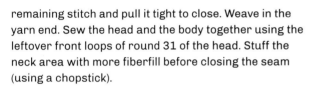

remaining stitch and pull it tight to close. Weave in the yarn end. Sew the head and the body together using the leftover front loops of round 31 of the head. Stuff the neck area with more fiberfill before closing the seam (using a chopstick).

JUMPSUIT

✳ *in jeans blue yarn, with a 4 steel / 1.75 mm crochet hook*

> **Note:** *Try the jumpsuit on as you go, we want it to fit like a soft glove.*

Ch 66 and join with a slst to make a circle. Make sure the chain isn't twisted.
Rnd 1: sc in all 66 ch [66]
> **Note:** *Try it on, the circle should fit the body nicely underneath the striped shirt. If it's too tight, consider using a bigger hook. If it's too loose, you might want to use a smaller hook.*

Rnd 2 – 8: sc in all 66 st [66] (picture 2)
Rnd 9: sc in next 5 st, (inc in next st, sc in next 10 st) repeat 5 times, inc in next st, sc in next 5 st [72]
Rnd 10 – 19: sc in all 72 st [72]
Rnd 20: sc in next 5 st, (dec, sc in next 10 st) repeat 5 times, dec, sc in next 5 st [66]
Rnd 21 – 26: sc in all 66 st [66]
Rnd 27: (sc in next 9 st, dec) repeat 6 times [60]
Rnd 28 – 31: sc in all 60 st [60]
Rnd 32: (slst in next 15 st, sc in next 15 st) repeat 2 times [60]
Fasten off, leaving a long tail for sewing. Put the jumpsuit on the body. There are two slst sections in round 32, these create the edges of the jumpsuit legs, so

make sure they're nicely lined up with the legs. Sew the remaining stitches between the legs (2 sections of 15 sc stitches each) closed (picture 3).

JUMPSUIT STRAP

✳ *in jeans blue yarn, with a 4 steel / 1.75 mm crochet hook*

Ch 61. Stitches are worked around both sides of the foundation chain.
Rnd 1: start in second ch from hook, sc in next 59 ch, 6 sc in next ch. Continue on the other side of the foundation chain, sc in next 58 ch, 5 sc in next ch [128] Fasten off, leaving a long tail for sewing. Sew the middle of the strap to the center of the jumpsuit at the back (picture 4). Sew both ends of the strap to the front of the jumpsuit, 2-3 rounds below the edge, using one or two strands of jeans blue yarn. Decorate the ends of the straps with tiny buttons.

JUMPSUIT POCKET

✳ *in jeans blue yarn, with a 4 steel / 1.75 mm crochet hook*

diagram 3 on page 135

Crochet in rows.
Row 1: start a magic ring with ch 2, 8 dc, ch 2, turn [8] Pull the magic ring tightly closed.
Row 2: dc inc in all 8 st, ch 2, turn [16]
Row 3: (dc in next st, dc inc in next st) repeat 8 times, ch 2, turn [24]
Row 4: (dc in next 2 st, dc inc in next st) repeat 8 times [32]

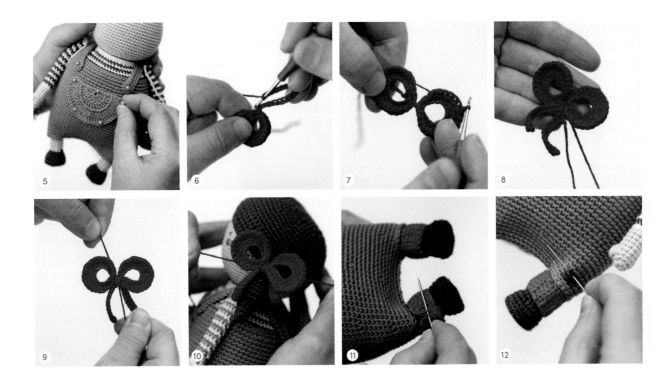

Optional row: slst in next 13 row-ends along the top, slst in next 32 st of Row 4 [45]
Fasten off, leaving a long tail for sewing. Sew the pocket to the center of the jumpsuit, at 5-7 rounds from the top (picture 5). Decorate it with two tiny buttons.

ARM
make 2, start in nude yarn

Rnd 1: start 5 sc in a magic ring [5]
Rnd 2: inc in all 5 st [10]
Rnd 3: sc in all 10 st [10]
Rnd 4: sc in next 4 st, 5-dc-bobble in next st, sc in next 5 st [10]
Rnd 5 – 9: sc in all 10 st [10]
Change to off-white yarn and crochet the next rounds in a stripe pattern, alternating off-white and graphite yarn with each round.
> **Note:** *Make sure the color change is at the inside of the arm, add a few sc or undo a few to get to this point.*

Rnd 10 – 29: sc in all 10 st [10]
Stuff only the lower half of the arms with fiberfill, so the arms don't stick out too much after sewing. Make a couple of additional sc or undo a few to get to the opposite side of the thumb. Flatten the arm and work the next round through both layers to close.
Rnd 30: sc in all 5 st [5]
Fasten off, leaving a yarn tail for sewing. Sew the arms to the sides of the body, on round 40, so the stripes on the sleeves match those on the shirt.

HAIR
in graphite yarn

Rnd 1: start 6 sc in a magic ring [6]
Rnd 2: inc in all 6 st [12]
Rnd 3: (sc in next st, inc in next st) repeat 6 times [18]
Rnd 4: sc in next st, (inc in next st, sc in next 2 st) repeat 5 times, inc in next st, sc in next st [24]
Rnd 5: (sc in next 3 st, inc in next st) repeat 6 times [30]
Rnd 6: sc in next 2 st, (inc in next st, sc in next 4 st)

repeat 5 times, inc in next st, sc in next 2 st [36]

Rnd 7: (sc in next 5 st, inc in next st) repeat 6 times [42]

Rnd 8: sc in next 3 st, (inc in next st, sc in next 6 st) repeat 5 times, inc in next st, sc in next 3 st [48]

Rnd 9: (sc in next 7 st, inc in next st) repeat 6 times [54]

Rnd 10: sc in next 4 st, (inc in next st, sc in next 8 st) repeat 5 times, inc in next st, sc in next 4 st [60]

Rnd 11: (sc in next 9 st, inc in next st) repeat 6 times [66]

Rnd 12: sc in next 5 st, (inc in next st, sc in next 10 st) repeat 5 times, inc in next st, sc in next 5 st [72]

Rnd 13 – 16: sc in all 72 st [72]

Rnd 17 – 21: hdc in next 17 st, sc in next st, slst in next st, sc in next st, hdc in next 17 st, sc in next 35 st [72]

Rnd 22: hdc in next 17 st, sc in next st, slst in next st, sc in next st, hdc in next 17 st, sc in next 33 st, slst in next 2 st [72]

Fasten off, leaving a long tail for sewing. Position the hair onto the head at an angle of approximately 45°. Secure it with pins. Split the yarn tail into strands and take one or two strands on a yarn needle. Mark the hair parting at the front top of the head with pins. Embroider a few short stitches through hair and head to fix the hair parting (see the pictures in Dad's pattern, page 22). Split another yarn piece into strands and use one or two strands to sew the back side of the hair to the head. Add fiberfill under the hair to give it some volume. Add the fiberfill in small amounts (we don't want Lula's hair to look like a mountain range). Make sure the hairdo looks smooth and even and has a nice shape. When you're happy with the way it looks, sew the front part of the hair to the forehead, using one or two strands of yarn, and weave in the yarn end.

PIGTAIL

✳ *make 2, in graphite yarn*

Rnd 1: start 6 sc in a magic ring [6]

Rnd 2: (sc in next st, inc in next st) repeat 3 times [9]

Rnd 3: sc in next st, (inc in next st, sc in next 2 st) repeat 2 times, inc in next st, sc in next st [12]

Rnd 4: (sc in next 3 st, inc in next st) repeat 3 times [15]

Rnd 5: sc in next 2 st, (inc in next st, sc in next 4 st) repeat 2 times, inc in next st, sc in next 2 st [18]

Rnd 6 – 8: sc in all 18 st [18]

Rnd 9: dec 3 times, sc in next 12 st [15]

Rnd 10: dec 3 times, sc in next 9 st [12]

Stuff the pigtail with fiberfill.

Rnd 11: (sc in next 2 st, dec) repeat 3 times [9]

Rnd 12: sc in all 9 st [9]

Rnd 13: (sc in next st, dec) repeat 3 times [6]

Fasten off, leaving a yarn tail. Using a yarn needle, weave the yarn tail through the front loop of each remaining stitch and pull it tight to close. Weave in the yarn end. Sew the pigtails to both sides of the head, right under the edge of the hair.

BOW

✳ *make 2, in red yarn*

Leave a long starting yarn tail. Ch 18 and join with a slst to make a circle. Make sure the chain isn't twisted.

Rnd 1: slst in next 6 ch, sc in next 6 ch, slst in next 6 ch [18]

Rnd 2: sc in next 3 st, (sc in next st, inc in next st) repeat 6 times, slst in next 3 st [24]

Rnd 3: sc in all 24 st [24]

Don't fasten off. Ch 18 and join with a slst to make a circle. Repeat Rnd 1-3 to make the second loop of the bow (pictures 6-7).

Don't fasten off. Continue crocheting the bow ends. (Ch 13, start in second ch from hook, sc in next 11 ch, slst in next ch) repeat 2 times (picture 8).

Fasten off, leaving a long yarn tail. Wrap the yarn tails a couple of times around the middle of the bow and tie a knot (picture 9). Use the yarn tails to tie the bows around Lula's pigtails. Weave in the yarn ends (picture 10).

EAR
✳ *make 2, in nude yarn*

Leave a long starting yarn tail.
Rnd 1: start 5 sc in a magic ring [5]
Pull the magic ring tightly closed and fasten off, leaving a tail for sewing. Sew the ears to both sides of the head, right under the edge of the hair. Weave in the yarn ends.

LEG WARMER
✳ *make 2, in fuchsia yarn*

Ch 6. Crochet in rows.
Row 1: start in second ch from hook, hdc in next 5 ch, ch 1, turn [5]
Row 2 – 11: hdc in next st, BLO hdc in next 3 st, hdc in next st, ch 1, turn [5]
Row 12: hdc in next st, BLO hdc in next 3 st, hdc in next st [5]

> **Note:** *Try the leg warmers on. You may want to make a row more or less depending on how firmly you crochet.*

Fasten off, leaving a long tail for sewing. Wrap the warmers around Lula's legs and sew the sides together (picture 11).

FINISHING TOUCHES

• Embroider the facial features. A water-soluble marker or sewing pins may come in handy to mark out the position of the eyes, mouth and cheeks first. The eyes are embroidered using one or two strands of graphite yarn or black embroidery thread. Position the eyes on round 16 of the head, with an interspace of approximately 17-18 stitches. Embroider the cheeks underneath the eyes using pink embroidery thread.

• Embroider patches on Lula's jumpsuit using graphite yarn (picture 12).

LULA'S LITTLE FRIEND

LEG
✳ *make 2, in brown yarn*

Rnd 1: start 6 sc in a magic ring [6]
Rnd 2 – 6: sc in all 6 st [6]
Fasten off on the first leg, leaving a yarn tail. Don't fasten off on the second leg. In the next round, we'll join both legs together and start crocheting the body.

BODY AND HEAD
✳ *continue in brown yarn*

Rnd 1: ch 3 and join to the first leg with a sc, sc next 5 st on the first leg, sc in all 3 ch, sc in next 6 st on the second leg, sc in the opposite side of next 3 ch [18]
Crochet an additional 3 sc to move the beginning of the round to the side of the body. This is the new beginning of the round.
Rnd 2: sc in all 18 st [18]
Rnd 3: sc in next st, (inc in next st, sc in next 2 st) repeat 5 times, inc in next st, sc in next st [24]
Rnd 4 – 8: sc in all 24 st [24]
Rnd 9: (sc in next 2 st, dec) repeat 6 times [18]
Rnd 10: (sc in next st, dec) repeat 6 times [12]
Rnd 11: sc in all 12 st [12]
Stuff the body firmly with fiberfill.
Rnd 12: inc in all 12 st [24]
Rnd 13 – 15: sc in all 24 st [24]
Rnd 16: (sc in next 2 st, dec) repeat 6 times [18]
Rnd 17: (sc in next st, dec) repeat 6 times [12]
Finish stuffing the body and head with fiberfill.

Rnd 18: dec 6 times [6]

Fasten off, leaving a yarn tail. Using a yarn needle, weave the yarn tail through the front loop of each remaining stitch and pull it tight to close. Weave in the yarn end.

ARM
* make 2, in brown yarn

Rnd 1: start 6 sc in a magic ring [6]
Rnd 2 – 9: sc in all 6 st [6]
Fasten off, leaving a yarn tail. Sew the arms to the sides of the body, right below the neck.

EAR
* make 2, in brown yarn

Rnd 1: start 6 sc in a magic ring [6]
Rnd 2 – 4: sc in all 6 st [6]
Fasten off, leaving a yarn tail. Sew the ears on top of the head, approximately between rounds 13 and 15.

MUZZLE
* in brown yarn

Rnd 1: start 6 sc in a magic ring [6]
Rnd 2: (sc in next st, inc in next st) repeat 3 times [9]
Rnd 3: sc in all 9 st [9]
Fasten off, leaving a yarn tail. Sew the muzzle to the center of the face. Embroider the teddy's nose and eyes using one or two strands of graphite yarn.

BOW
* in red yarn

Leave a long starting yarn tail.
Row 1: (ch 12, join with a slst to create a circle, sc in all 12 ch) repeat 2 times, (ch 6, sc in second ch from hook, sc in next 4 ch, slst in next ch) repeat 2 times. Fasten off, leaving a yarn tail. Wrap the yarn tails a few times around the middle of the bow and tie a knot. Tie the bow around teddy's neck. Weave in the yarn ends.

BO

Bo is Lula's little brother. He always walks around with his tortilla chip toy, he has a deep fascination for earthworms and loves to secretly dip his pacifier into Dad's morning frappuccino. He tries to follow his elder sister and her friends around, but he somehow always fails to join their adventures.

SKILL LEVEL

* *

SIZE

6.5" / 16.5 cm tall when made with the indicated yarn.

MATERIALS

- Fingering weight yarn in
  • red
  • black
  • nude
  • graphite
  • mustard yellow (leftover)
  • off-white (leftover)
- 7 steel / 1.5 mm crochet hook
- Scraps of black and pink yarn or embroidery thread for the embroidery
- Sewing needle
- Yarn needle
- Pins
- 4 buttons (diameter 0.4" / 1 cm) for the toy's wheels
- 2 flat buttons (diameter 0.8" / 2 cm) to strengthen the feet
- Approx. 4" / 10 cm of crafting wire
- Stitch markers
- Fiberfill for stuffing

Scan or visit
www.amigurumi.com/3904
to share pictures and find inspiration.

BODY

* *start in red yarn*

Rnd 1: start 6 sc in a magic ring [6]
Rnd 2: inc in all 6 st [12]
Rnd 3: (sc in next st, inc in next st) repeat 6 times [18]
Rnd 4: sc in next st, (inc in next st, sc in next 2 st) repeat 5 times, inc in next st, sc in next st [24]
Rnd 5: (sc in next 3 st, inc in next st) repeat 6 times [30]
Rnd 6: sc in next 2 st, (inc in next st, sc in next 4 st) repeat 5 times, inc in next st, sc in next 2 st [36]
Rnd 7: (sc in next 5 st, inc in next st) repeat 6 times [42]
Rnd 8: sc in next 3 st, (inc in next st, sc in next 6 st) repeat 5 times, inc in next st, sc in next 3 st [48]
Rnd 9: (sc in next 7 st, inc in next st) repeat 6 times [54]
Rnd 10: sc in next 4 st, (inc in next st, sc in next 8 st) repeat 5 times, inc in next st, sc in next 4 st [60]
Rnd 11 – 16: sc in all 60 st [60]
Rnd 17: (sc in next 3 st, dec) repeat 12 times [48]
Change to black yarn.
Rnd 18: BLO sc in all 48 st [48]
Rnd 19: spike st in all 48 st [48]
Rnd 20: BLO (sc in next 3 st, inc in next st) repeat 12 times [60]
Rnd 21 – 22: sc in all 60 st [60]
Rnd 23: sc in next 4 st, (dec, sc in next 8 st) repeat 5 times, dec, sc in next 4 st [54]
Rnd 24 – 26: sc in all 54 st [54]
Rnd 27: (sc in next 7 st, dec) repeat 6 times [48]
Rnd 28 – 30: sc in all 48 st [48]
Rnd 31: sc in next 3 st, (dec, sc in next 6 st) repeat 5 times, dec, sc in next 3 st [42]
Rnd 32: sc in all 42 st [42]
Rnd 33: (sc in next 5 st, dec) repeat 6 times [36]
Rnd 34: sc in next 2 st, (dec, sc in next 4 st) repeat 5 times, dec, sc in next 2 st [30]
Fasten off, leaving a long tail for sewing.
Stuff the body very firmly with fiberfill.

HEAD

* *in nude yarn*

Rnd 1: start 6 sc in a magic ring [6]
Rnd 2: inc in all 6 st [12]

Rnd 3: (sc in next st, inc in next st) repeat 6 times [18]
Rnd 4: sc in next st, (inc in next st, sc in next 2 st) repeat 5 times, inc in next st, sc in next st [24]
Rnd 5: (sc in next 3 st, inc in next st) repeat 6 times [30]
Rnd 6: sc in next 2 st, (inc in next st, sc in next 4 st) repeat 5 times, inc in next st, sc in next 2 st [36]
Rnd 7: (sc in next 5 st, inc in next st) repeat 6 times [42]
Rnd 8: sc in next 3 st, (inc in next st, sc in next 6 st) repeat 5 times, inc in next st, sc in next 3 st [48]
Rnd 9: (sc in next 7 st, inc in next st) repeat 6 times [54]
Rnd 10: sc in next 4 st, (inc in next st, sc in next 8 st) repeat 5 times, inc in next st, sc in next 4 st [60]
Rnd 11 – 25: sc in all 60 st [60]
Rnd 26: sc in next 4 st, (dec, sc in next 8 st) repeat 5 times, dec, sc in next 4 st [54]
Rnd 27: (sc in next 7 st, dec) repeat 6 times [48]
Stuff the head with fiberfill and continue stuffing as you go.
Rnd 28: sc in next 3 st, (dec, sc in next 6 st) repeat 5 times, dec, sc in next 3 st [42]
Rnd 29: (sc in next 5 st, dec) repeat 6 times [36]
Rnd 30: sc in next 2 st, (dec, sc in next 4 st) repeat 5 times, dec, sc in next 2 st [30]
Rnd 31: BLO (sc in next 3 st, dec) repeat 6 times [24]
Rnd 32: sc in next st, (dec, sc in next 2 st) repeat 5 times, dec, sc in next st [18]
Finish stuffing the head very firmly.
Rnd 33: (dec, sc in next st) repeat 6 times [12]
Rnd 34: dec 6 times [6]
Fasten off, leaving a yarn tail. Using a yarn needle, weave the yarn tail through the front loop of each remaining stitch and pull it tight to close. Weave in the yarn end. Sew the head and the body together using the leftover front loops of round 30 of the head. Stuff the neck area with more fiberfill before closing the seam (using a chopstick).

LEG
* make 2, start in mustard yellow yarn

Rnd 1: start 6 sc in a magic ring [6]
Rnd 2: inc in all 6 st [12]
Rnd 3: BLO sc in all 12 st [12]
Rnd 4: sc in all 12 st [12]
> **Note:** Insert a flat button inside the foot at this point.

> It's important to keep the soles flat as we want them to have the same shape as cute little hooves.

Rnd 5: (dec, sc in next 2 st) repeat 3 times [9]
Rnd 6 – 9: sc in all 9 st [9]
Change to red yarn. Stuff the leg firmly with fiberfill and continue stuffing as you go.
Rnd 10: sc in all 9 st [9]
Rnd 11: inc in all 9 st [18]
Fasten off, leaving a long tail for sewing. Sew the legs to the bottom of the body, approximately between rounds 4 and 8 (picture 1).

ARM
* make 2, start in nude yarn

Rnd 1: start 6 sc in a magic ring [6]
Rnd 2 – 5: sc in all 6 st [6]
Change to black yarn.
> **Note:** Make sure the color change is at the inside of the arm, add a few sc or undo a few to get to this point.

Rnd 6: sc in all 6 st [6]
Rnd 7: FLO inc in all 6 st [12]
Rnd 8 – 20: sc in all 12 st [12]
Stuff only the lower half of the arm with fiberfill, so the arms don't stick out too much after sewing. Flatten the arm and work the next round through both layers to close.
Rnd 21: sc in all 6 st [6]
Fasten off, leaving a yarn tail for sewing. Sew the arms to the sides of the body, on round 32.

HAIR
* in graphite yarn

Diagram 8 on page 135

Bo's hair is made like a beanie, with the front side shorter than the back and showing some individual hair strands for the fringe.
> **Note:** Try to crochet the hair loosely or move up a crochet hook size.

Leave a long starting yarn tail. Ch 21. Crochet in rows.
Row 1: start in second ch from hook, slst in next 4 ch,

sc in next 4 ch, hdc in next 12 ch, ch 1, turn [20]

Row 2: hdc in next st, BLO hdc in next 11 st, BLO sc in next 4 st, BLO slst in next 3 st, slst in next st, ch 1, turn [20]

Row 3: slst in next st, BLO slst in next 3 st, BLO sc in next 4 st, BLO hdc in next 11 st, hdc in next st, ch 1, turn [20]

Row 4 – 8: repeat rows 2 and 3 alternately [20]

Row 9: slst in next st, BLO slst in next 3 st, BLO sc in next 4 st, BLO hdc in next 5 st, hdc in next st, ch 1, turn [14] Don't finish this row. Continue working on these 14 stitches only.

Row 10: hdc in next st, BLO hdc in next 5 st, BLO sc in next 4 st, BLO slst in next 3 st, slst in next st, ch 1, turn [14]

Row 11 – 12: repeat rows 9 and 10 [14]

Row 13: slst in next st, BLO slst in next 3 st, BLO sc in next 4 st, BLO hdc in next 2 st, slst in next st, ch 4, turn [11 + 4 ch]

Row 14: start in second ch from hook, hdc in next 3 ch, BLO hdc in next 3 st, BLO sc in next 4 st, BLO slst in next 3 st, slst in next st, ch 1, turn [14]

Row 15 – 18: repeat rows 13 and 14 alternately [14]

Row 19: slst in next st, BLO slst in next 3 st, BLO sc in next 4 st, BLO hdc in next 5 st, hdc in next st, ch 1, turn [14]

Row 20: hdc in next st, BLO hdc in next 5 st, BLO sc in next 4 st, BLO slst in next 3 st, slst in next st, ch 1, turn [14]

Row 21 – 26: repeat rows 19 and 20 alternately [14]

Row 27: slst in next st, BLO slst in next 3 st, BLO sc in next 4 st, BLO hdc in next 5 st, hdc in next st, ch 7, turn [14 + 7 ch]

Row 28: start in second ch from hook, hdc in next 6 ch, hdc in next st, BLO hdc in next 5 st, BLO sc in next 4 st, BLO slst in next 3 st, slst in next st, ch 1, turn [20]

Row 29: slst in next st, BLO slst in next 3 st, BLO sc in next 4 st, BLO hdc in next 11 st, hdc in next st, ch 1, turn [20]

Row 30: hdc in next st, BLO hdc in next 11 st, BLO sc in next 4 st, BLO slst in next 3 st, slst in next st, ch 1, turn [20]

Row 31 – 38: repeat rows 29 and 30 alternately [20] Don't fasten off, but continue crocheting the crown of the hair. Continue crocheting in rounds.

Rnd 1: join the end of row 38 with the beginning of row 1 with a slst (pictures 2-3). Work sc in all row-ends around the top [21] (pictures 4)

> *Note: If you have 1 st more or less in this round, make an extra decrease or skip one just to make it easier to work the last rounds. It's all good as long as it looks neat.*

Rnd 2: (dec, sc in next st) repeat 7 times [14]

Rnd 3: dec 7 times [7]

Fasten off, leaving a very long yarn tail. Using a yarn needle, weave the yarn tail through the front loop of each remaining stitch and pull it tight to close. Don't fasten off but continue making the hair tuft.

Hair tuft: ch 7, start in second ch from hook, slst in next 6 ch, ch 5, start in second ch from hook, slst in next 4 ch.

Fasten off and weave in the yarn end. Using the starting yarn tail, sew row 38 and row 1 of the hair together. Position the hair on the head, with the shorter fringe at the front. Smoothen the hair to make sure it enwraps the head nicely. Secure it with pins in this position. Split a piece of graphite yarn into strands and take one or two strands on a yarn needle to sew the hair to the head (picture 5).

COLLAR
* in off-white yarn

Diagram 7 on page 135

Ch 5. Crochet in rows.
Row 1: start in second ch from hook, sc in next 4 ch, ch 10, start in second ch from hook, sc in next 4 ch, ch 2, turn [8]

Row 2: dc in the same sc as ch 2, dc in next 2 st, 6 dc in next st, dc in next 3 st, skip 2 ch, slst in next ch, skip 2 ch, dc in next 3 st, 6 dc in next st, dc in next 3 st [25]
In the next row, we'll make the ties.
Row 3: ch 25, start in second ch from hook, slst in next 24 ch, sc in next 11 st along the top of the collar, ch 25, start in second ch from hook, slst in next 24 ch.
Fasten off and weave in the yarn ends.

PACIFIER
* in mustard yellow yarn

Rnd 1: start 8 sc in a magic ring [8]
Rnd 2: inc in all 8 st [16]
Rnd 3: slst in all 16 st [16]
Fasten off and weave in the yarn end on the wrong side of your work.
To make the pacifier ring, make a ring out of crafting wire that matches the size of the pacifier guard. You can make it by wrapping it around a round object (picture 6). Work sc all around the piece (picture 7). Fasten off, leaving a long tail for sewing. Sew the ring to the pacifier guard.

EAR
* make 2, in nude yarn

Leave a long starting yarn tail.
Rnd 1: start 5 sc in a magic ring [5]
Pull the magic ring tightly closed and fasten off, leaving a long tail for sewing. Sew the ears to both sides of the head, right under the edge of the fringe. Weave in the yarn ends.

TORTILLA CHIP ON WHEELS
* in mustard yellow yarn

Rnd 1: start 6 sc in a magic ring [6]
Rnd 2: (sc in next st, inc in next st) repeat 3 times [9]
Rnd 3: (sc in next 2 st, inc in next st) repeat 3 times [12]

Rnd 4: (sc in next 5 st, inc in next st) repeat 2 times [14]
Rnd 5: (sc in next 6 st, inc in next st) repeat 2 times [16]
Rnd 6: (sc in next 7 st, inc in next st) repeat 2 times [18]
Rnd 7: (sc in next 8 st, inc in next st) repeat 2 times [20]
Rnd 8: (sc in next 9 st, inc in next st) repeat 2 times [22]
Rnd 9: (sc in next 10 st, inc in next st) repeat 2 times [24]
Fasten off, leaving a long tail for sewing. Stuff the toy lightly, flatten the bottom part and sew the gap closed. Weave in the yarn end. Sew two flat buttons on each bottom side of the toy, mimicking wheels. Embroider a funny face on the toy using one or two strands of black and red yarn.

FINISHING TOUCHES

- Randomly embroider French knots all over the lower part of Bo's body using off-white yarn. Alternatively, you can use tiny white buttons or white beads to create polka dots, it'll look fun this way too (picture 8).
- Embroider the facial features. A water-soluble marker or sewing pins may come in handy to mark out the position of the eyes, nose and cheeks first. The eyes are embroidered using one or two strands of graphite yarn or black embroidery thread. Position the eyes just 1 round below the fringe, with an interspace of approximately 16-18 stitches. Embroider the nose in between the eyes using pink embroidery thread. Embroider the cheeks underneath the eyes using pink embroidery thread.
- Attach the pacifier to the center of the face. You can sew it on, but don't hesitate to use a glue gun if you have one, it's much easier.
- Put the collar around Bo's neck and tie the straps at the back.
- Make a leash for the tortilla chip toy using a piece of red yarn. Pull the yarn end through Bo's hand using a yarn needle. Tie a double knot at the end of the leash, so Bo will never lose his tortilla toy.

OPA

Opa is the grandfather of Lula and Bo and ever since he retired, he's been enjoying a never-ending vacation. He's always dressed as if he's on the beach. We forgive him his fashion choices though, since his Hawaiian shirts do cheer up everyone around him.

SKILL LEVEL

* *

SIZE

9" / 22.5 cm tall when made with the indicated yarn.

MATERIALS

- Fingering weight yarn in:
  • peach
  • red
  • off-white
  • pink
  • jeans blue
  • mauve
  • green (leftover)
  • brown (leftover)
  • mustard yellow (leftover)
  • graphite (leftover)
- 7 and 4 steel / 1.5 and 1.75 mm crochet hooks
- Scraps of green, brown, red, black, white and pink yarn or embroidery thread for the embroidery
- Sewing needle
- Yarn needle
- Pins
- 6 tiny buttons or beads (diameter 1/16" / 2 mm) for the swimsuit straps and the shirt
- 8" / 20 cm of red crafting wire to make the glasses
- A short piece of florist wire or a paperclip for the radio antenna
- A piece of plastic or cardboard to reinforce the radio
- Stitch markers
- Fiberfill for stuffing

Scan or visit
www.amigurumi.com/3905
to share pictures and find inspiration.

Note: *All parts are worked with a 7 steel / 1.5 mm crochet hook, except for the oversized shorts and the shirt (these are worked with a 4 steel / 1.75 mm crochet hook).*

LEG

* *make 2, start in mustard yellow yarn*

Ch 7. Stitches are worked around both sides of the foundation chain.
Rnd 1: start in second ch from hook, sc in next 5 ch, 4 sc in next ch. Continue on the other side of the foundation chain, sc in next 4 ch, 3 sc in next ch [16]
Rnd 2: inc in next st, sc in next 4 st, inc in next 4 st, sc in next 4 st, inc in next 3 st [24]
Rnd 3: BLO sc in all 24 st [24]
Rnd 4: spike st in all 24 st [24]
Change to graphite yarn.
Rnd 5: BLO slst in all 24 st [24] (picture 1)
Rnd 6: work this round in BLO, sc in next 6 st, dec 6 times, sc in next 6 st [18]
Rnd 7: sc in next 6 st, dec 3 times, sc in next 6 st [15] (picture 2)
Change to off-white yarn.
Rnd 8 – 9: sc in all 15 st [15]
Change to graphite yarn.
Rnd 10: sc in all 15 st [15]
Change to off-white yarn.
Rnd 11 – 12: sc in all 15 st [15]
Change to graphite yarn. Stuff the leg firmly with fiberfill and continue stuffing as you go.
Rnd 13: sc in all 15 st [15]
Change to off-white yarn.
Rnd 14: sc in all 15 st [15]
Rnd 15: BLO sc in all 15 st [15]
Rnd 16: spike st in all 15 st [15]
Change to peach yarn.
Rnd 17: BLO sc in all 15 st [15]
Rnd 18 – 39: sc in all 15 st [15]
Change to off-white yarn.
Rnd 40: BLO sc in all 15 st [15]
Rnd 41: spike st in all 15 st [15]
Change to jeans blue yarn.
Rnd 42: BLO sc in all 15 st [15]
Rnd 43: sc in all 15 st [15]

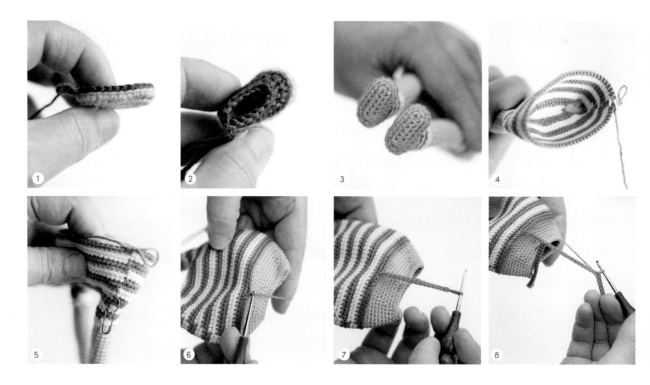

Fasten off and weave in the yarn end on the first leg. Don't fasten off on the second leg and change to off-white yarn.

Rnd 44: sc in next 6 st on the second leg (the last stitch should be on the side of the leg, crochet an additional 1-2 st or undo a few to reach this point) [6] Leave the remaining stitches unworked.

Make sure that the legs are stuffed very firmly with fiberfill (picture 3). It's very important because Opa likes to show off his assets. In the next round, we'll start crocheting the body.

BODY

 ✳ *continue in off-white yarn*

Rnd 1: ch 9 and join to the first leg with a sc (make sure the feet point forwards), sc in next 14 st on the first leg, sc in next 9 ch, sc in next 9 st on the second leg (if you had to add or undo 1-2 stitches at the beginning of the round, make sure to take it into account at the end) [48]

> **Note:** *You don't need military precision here because the toy is pretty big. If you miscalculated and missed*

a stitch or made an extra one, don't get upset, just make an increase or a decrease in the next round to reach the correct number of stitches.

Rnd 2: (sc in next 7 st, inc in next st) repeat 6 times [54] Change to jeans blue yarn.

Rnd 3: sc in next 4 st, (inc in next st, sc in next 8 st) repeat 5 times, inc in next st, sc in next 4 st [60]

Rnd 4: (sc in next 9 st, inc in next st) repeat 6 times [66] Change to off-white yarn and crochet the next rounds in a stripe pattern, alternating off-white and jeans blue yarn every 2 rounds (pictures 4-5).

Rnd 5 – 22: sc in all 66 st [66]
Continue in jeans blue yarn.

Rnd 23: sc in all 66 st [66]

Rnd 24: sc in next 10 st, (dec, sc in next 20 st) repeat 2 times, dec, sc in next 10 st [63]
Change to peach yarn, but don't fasten off the jeans blue yarn just yet and leave it hanging on the outside of your work.

Rnd 25: BLO (sc in next 19 st, dec) repeat 3 times [60]

Rnd 26: sc in next 9 st, (dec, sc in next 18 st) repeat 2 times, dec, sc in next 9 st [57]

Rnd 27: (sc in next 17 st, dec) repeat 3 times [54]
Rnd 28: sc in next 8 st, (dec, sc in next 16 st) repeat
2 times, dec, sc in next 8 st [51]
Rnd 29: (sc in next 15 st, dec) repeat 3 times [48]
Rnd 30: sc in next 7 st, (dec, sc in next 14 st) repeat
2 times, dec, sc in next 7 st [45]
Rnd 31: (sc in next 13 st, dec) repeat 3 times [42]
Rnd 32: sc in next 6 st, (dec, sc in next 12 st) repeat
2 times, dec, sc in next 6 st [39]
Rnd 33: (sc in next 11 st, dec) repeat 3 times [36]
Fasten off, leaving a long tail for sewing.

SWIMSUIT STRAPS
* in jeans blue yarn

Hold the body with the opening away from you. Take
the jeans blue yarn on the outside of your work on your
crochet hook and start in the unworked front loop of
round 24 where the yarn appears.
Rnd 1: FLO slst in next 16 st (make sure you end up at
the center of the back, crochet an additional 1-2 slst or
undo a few if needed (picture 6)), ch 29 (picture 7), start
in second ch from hook, slst in next 24 ch, ch 25, start in
second ch from hook, slst in next 24 ch (picture 8), sc in
next 4 ch, FLO slst in next 47 st.
Fasten off and weave in the yarn end. Stuff the body firmly
with fiberfill.

HEAD
* in peach yarn

Rnd 1: start 6 sc in a magic ring [6]
Rnd 2: inc in all 6 st [12]
Rnd 3: (sc in next st, inc in next st) repeat 6 times [18]
Rnd 4: sc in next st, (inc in next st, sc in next 2 st) repeat
5 times, inc in next st, sc in next st [24]
Rnd 5: (sc in next 3 st, inc in next st) repeat 6 times [30]
Rnd 6: sc in next 2 st, (inc in next st, sc in next 4 st)
repeat 5 times, inc in next st, sc in next 2 st [36]
Rnd 7: (sc in next 5 st, inc in next st) repeat 6 times [42]
Rnd 8: sc in next 3 st, (inc in next st, sc in next 6 st)
repeat 5 times, inc in next st, sc in next 3 st [48]
Rnd 9: (sc in next 7 st, inc in next st) repeat 6 times [54]

Rnd 10: sc in next 4 st, (inc in next st, sc in next 8 st)
repeat 5 times, inc in next st, sc in next 4 st [60]
Rnd 11: (sc in next 9 st, inc in next st) repeat 6 times [66]
Rnd 12 – 25: sc in all 66 st [66]
Rnd 26: (sc in next 9 st, dec) repeat 6 times [60]
Rnd 27: sc in next 4 st, (dec, sc in next 8 st) repeat
5 times, dec, sc in next 4 st [54]
Rnd 28: (sc in next 7 st, dec) repeat 6 times [48]
Stuff the head with fiberfill and continue stuffing as
you go.
Rnd 29: sc in next 3 st, (dec, sc in next 6 st) repeat
5 times, dec, sc in next 3 st [42]
Rnd 30: (sc in next 5 st, dec) repeat 6 times [36]
Rnd 31: work this round in BLO, sc in next 2 st, (dec,
sc in next 4 st) repeat 5 times, dec, sc in next 2 st [30]
Rnd 32: (sc in next 3 st, dec) repeat 6 times [24]
Rnd 33: sc in next st, (dec, sc in next 2 st) repeat
5 times, dec, sc in next st [18]
Finish stuffing the head very firmly.
Rnd 34: (dec, sc in next st) repeat 6 times [12]
Rnd 35: dec 6 times [6]
Fasten off, leaving a yarn tail. Using a yarn needle, weave

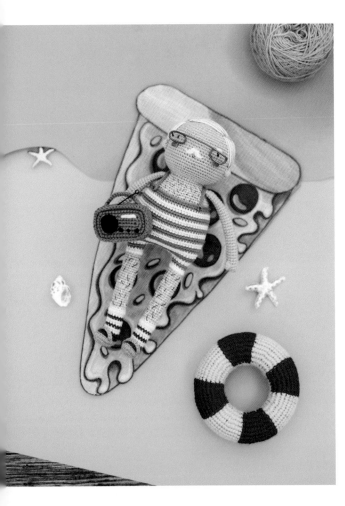

the yarn tail through the front loop of each remaining stitch and pull it tight to close. Weave in the yarn end. Sew the head and the body together using the leftover front loops of round 30 of the head. Stuff the neck and shoulder area with more fiberfill before closing the seam (using a chopstick).

ARM

* make 2, in peach yarn

Rnd 1: start 5 sc in a magic ring [5]
Rnd 2: inc in all 5 st [10]
Rnd 3: sc in all 10 st [10]
Rnd 4: sc in next 4 st, 5-dc-bobble in next st, sc in next

5 st [10]
Rnd 5 – 31: sc in all 10 st [10]
Stuff only the lower half of the arms with fiberfill, so the arms don't stick out too much after sewing. Make a couple of additional sc or undo a few to get to the opposite side of the thumb. Flatten the arm and work the next round through both layers to close.
Rnd 32: sc in all 5 st [5]
Fasten off, leaving a yarn tail for sewing. Sew the arms to the sides of the body, approximately between rounds 31 and 32.
Sew the ends of the swimsuit straps to the front of the swimsuit and decorate them with tiny buttons or beads.

EAR

* make 2, in peach yarn

Leave a long starting yarn tail.
Rnd 1: start 5 sc in a magic ring [5]
Pull the magic ring tightly closed and fasten off, leaving a long tail for sewing.

SANDAL STRAP

* make 2, in mustard yellow yarn

Leave a long starting yarn tail. Ch 11. Crochet in rows.
Row 1: start in second ch from hook, slst in next 10 ch [10]
Fasten off, leaving a long tail for sewing. Sew the straps to the feet and weave in the yarn ends.

FINISHING TOUCHES

• To make the hair, pin or draw its position using a water-soluble marker or sewing pins. Opa has a hairdo commonly called "lake in the woods". It consists of a larger back part (10-12 rounds high and 36 stitches wide) and a smaller front part covering about 30 % of the bald spot. Cover the back of the head using one or two strands of off-white yarn, making long stitches between rounds 8-9 and 19-21 of the head. Don't pass the needle through the head (this can change the head shape), but use only the front loops or the

spaces between the stitches for sewing. Next, cover approximately 30% of the bald spot in the same way. We patiently embroidered two layers to make Opa's hair more voluminous (picture 9). To make the hair more pronounced, you can add extra strands using graphite yarn (pictures 10-11).

- Sew the ears to both sides of the head, right under the edge of the hair, approximately between rounds 19-20.
- Embroider the facial features. A water-soluble marker or sewing pins may come in handy to mark out the position of the eyes, eyebrows, moustache and cheeks first. Embroider the eyes and mouth using one or two strands of graphite yarn or black embroidery thread and the eyebrows and moustache using one or two strands of off-white yarn or white embroidery thread. The eyes are embroidered on round 16 of the head, with an interspace of approximately 14-16 stitches. Embroider the cheeks underneath the eyes using pink embroidery thread.
- To make the glasses, wrap a piece of crafting wire around a small rectangular object. Skip a section about the distance between the eyes, then wrap the wire around the rectangular object again (picture 12). There should be approximately 0.8" / 2 cm left on the ends for the earpieces. Cut off the excess wire. Insert the earpieces into the head at 3-4 stitches from each eye (picture 13).
- Make a couple of stitches (2-3 stitches wide) on each leg using peach yarn, at 8-10 rounds above the edges of the socks, to mimic the knees.
- Make some random stitches using single strands of graphite and off-white yarn to give Opa some chest and leg hair.

OVERSIZED BOARD SHORTS

* *start in red yarn, using a 4 steel / 1.75 mm crochet hook*

> **Note:** *If you want to make the board shorts in one color, you can replace the bobble stitches with regular sc.*

Ch 66 and join with a slst to make a circle. Make sure the chain isn't twisted.

Rnd 1: sc in all 66 ch [66]

> **Note:** *Try it on, the circle should fit the body nicely underneath the arms. If it's too tight, consider using a bigger hook. If it's too loose, you might want to use a smaller hook.*

Rnd 2: (sc in next 10 st, inc in next st) repeat 6 times [72]

Rnd 3: sc in all 72 st [72]

Make the 3-dc-bobbles in all of the next rounds using off-white yarn (you can carry it on the wrong side of your work instead of fastening off every time). Change back to red yarn for all other stitches.

Rnd 4: sc in next 3 st, (3-dc-bobble in next st, sc in next 5 st) repeat 11 times, 3-dc-bobble in next st, sc in next 2 st [72]

Rnd 5 – 7: sc in all 72 st [72]

Rnd 8: sc in next st, (3-dc-bobble in next st, sc in next 5 st) repeat 11 times, 3-dc-bobble in next st, sc in next 4 st [72]

Rnd 9 – 11: sc in all 72 st [72]

Rnd 12: (sc in next 5 st, 3-dc-bobble in next st) repeat

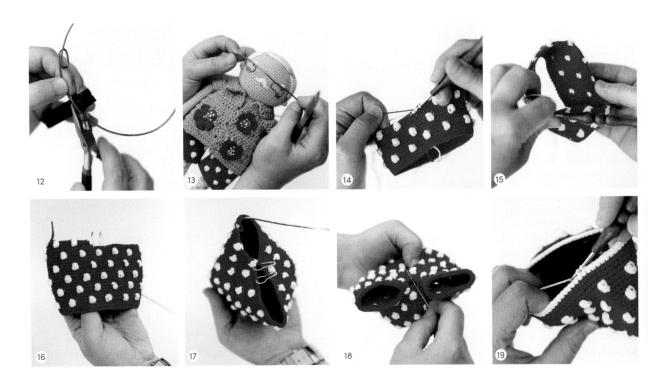

12 times [72] (pictures 14-15)

Rnd 13 – 15: sc in all 72 st [72]

Rnd 16: sc in next 3 st, (3-dc-bobble in next st, sc in next 5 st) repeat 11 times, 3-dc-bobble in next st, sc in next 2 st [72]

Rnd 17 – 19: sc in all 72 st [72]

Rnd 20: sc in next st, (3-dc-bobble in next st, sc in next 5 st) repeat 11 times, 3-dc-bobble in next st, sc in next 4 st [72]

Rnd 21 – 22: sc in all 72 st [72]

To make the shorts legs, divide your work in four parts: 33 stitches for the first shorts leg, 3 stitches for the central front part, 33 stitches for the second shorts leg and 3 stitches for the central back part. Continue working the first shorts leg.

FIRST SHORTS LEG

* continue in red yarn, using the off-white yarn for the 3-dc-bobbles

Rnd 23: sc in next 33 st, skip the remaining stitches [33]

Continue working on these 33 stitches only.

Rnd 24: sc in next st, (3-dc-bobble in next st, sc in next 5 st) repeat 5 times, 3-dc-bobble in next st, sc in next st [33] (pictures 16-17)

Rnd 25 – 27: sc in all 33 st [33]

Rnd 28: (sc in next 5 st, 3-dc-bobble in next st) repeat 5 times, sc in next 3 st [33]

Fasten off the off-white yarn.

Rnd 29 – 30: sc in all 33 st [33]

Rnd 31: slst in all 33 st [33]

Fasten off and weave in the yarn end.

SECOND SHORTS LEG

* continue in red yarn, using the off-white yarn for the 3-dc-bobbles

Leave a starting yarn tail. Pull up a loop of red yarn in the fourth stitch next to the first shorts leg on round 22.

Rnd 23: sc in next 33 st, skip the remaining stitches [33]

Continue working on these 33 stitches only.

Rnd 24: sc in next 2 st, (3-dc-bobble in next st, sc in next

5 st) repeat 5 times, 3-dc-bobble in next st [33]

Rnd 25 – 27: sc in all 33 st [33]

Rnd 28: (sc in next 5 st, 3-dc-bobble in next st) repeat 5 times, sc in next 3 st [33]

Fasten off the off-white yarn.

Rnd 29 – 30: sc in all 33 st [33]

Rnd 31: slst in all 33 st [33]

Fasten off and weave in the yarn end. Using the starting yarn tail of the second shorts legs, sew the central front and central back part of the shorts (the gap between the legs) closed (picture 18).

WAISTBAND
* in off-white yarn

Pull up a loop of off-white yarn in round 1 of the shorts, at the back.

Rnd 1: sc in all 66 st [66]

Rnd 2: slst in all 66 st [66] (picture 19)

Fasten off and weave in the yarn end.

HIDEOUS SHIRT
* in pink yarn, using a 4 steel / 1.75 mm crochet hook

> **Note:** Try the shirt on as you go: it should be a little bit tight at the top (so you can see some chest hair) and a bit looser from the chest down (so you're able to button it).

Ch 43. Crochet in rows.

Row 1: start in second ch from hook, sc in next 42 ch, ch 2, turn [42]

Row 2: hdc in all 42 st, ch 2, turn [42]

Row 3: (hdc in next 5 st, hdc2tog) repeat 6 times, ch 1, turn [36]

Row 4: sc in all 36 st, ch 2, turn [36]

Check to see if the collar hugs the neck nicely.

Row 5: (hdc in next 6 st, hdc inc in next st, hdc in next 4 st, hdc inc in next st, hdc in next 6 st) repeat 2 times, ch 2, turn [40]

Row 6: (hdc in next 6 st, hdc inc in next 2 st, hdc in next 4 st, hdc inc in next 2 st, hdc in next 6 st) repeat 2 times, ch 2, turn [48]

Row 7: (hdc in next 6 st, hdc inc in next 2 st, hdc in next

8 st, hdc inc in next 2 st, hdc in next 6 st) repeat 2 times, ch 2, turn [56]

Row 8: (hdc in next 6 st, hdc inc in next 2 st, hdc in next 12 st, hdc inc in next 2 st, hdc in next 6 st) repeat 2 times, ch 2, turn [64]

Row 9: hdc in next 3 st, hdc inc in next 2 st, hdc in next 3 st, ch 8, skip next 10 st (to make the first armhole), hdc in next 28 st, ch 8, skip next 10 st (to make the second armhole), hdc in next 3 st, hdc inc in next 2 st, hdc in next 3 st, ch 2, turn [48 + 16 ch] (picture 20)

Row 10: hdc in next 10 st, hdc in next 8 ch, hdc in next 3 st, (hdc inc in next st, hdc in next 6 st) repeat 3 times, hdc inc in next st, hdc in next 3 st, hdc in next 8 ch, hdc in next 10 st, ch 2, turn [68] (picture 21)

Row 11 – 21: hdc in all 68 st, ch 2, turn [68]

Row 22: hdc in all 68 st [68]

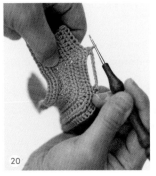
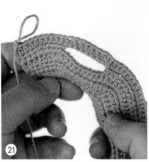

Fasten off and weave in the yarn end on the wrong side of your work (picture 22).

SLEEVES
* in pink yarn

Pull up a loop of pink yarn in a stitch at the bottom center of the armhole (picture 23).
Rnd 1: sc in next 4 st, sc in the side post of the armhole, sc in next 2 st, hdc in next 6 st, sc in next 2 st, sc in the side post of the armhole, sc in next 4 st [20]
Rnd 2 – 3: sc in next 7 st, hdc in next 6 st, sc in next 7 st [20]
Fasten off and weave in the yarn end. Make the second sleeve in the same way.

FLORAL PRINTS
diagrams 11 and 12 on page 135
Make as many elements as you wish.

PALM LEAVES
* in green yarn

Leave a starting yarn tail.
Row 1: (ch 8, start in second ch from hook, slst in next ch, sc in next ch, hdc in next ch, dc in next 2 ch, hdc in next ch, sc in next ch) repeat 4 times.
Fasten off, leaving a long tail for sewing.

PALM TRUNK
* in brown yarn

Leave a starting yarn tail. Ch 9. Crochet in rows.
Row 1: start in second ch from hook, slst in next ch, sc in next 2 ch, hdc in next 2 ch, dc in next 3 ch.
Fasten off, leaving a long tail for sewing.

LARGE FLOWER
* in red yarn

Rnd 1: start 5 sc in a magic ring [5]
Rnd 2: inc in all 5 st [10]
Rnd 3: (ch 4, 3 tr in next st, ch 4, sc in next st) repeat 5 times.
Fasten off and weave in the yarn end on the wrong side of your work.

SMALL FLOWER
* in red yarn

Rnd 1: start 5 sc in a magic ring [5]
Rnd 2: inc in all 5 st [10]
Rnd 3: (ch 3, 3 dc in next st, ch 3, sc in next st) repeat 5 times.
Fasten off and weave in the yarn end on the wrong side of your work. Flatten the shirt and arrange all the parts of your "print" nicely on the front side. Pin and sew them in place using a yarn needle and single strands of yarn or embroidery thread in matching colors. Weave

in the yarn ends on the wrong side of your work. Embroider a few small French knots in the center of each flower using off-white yarn. Embroider a few larger ones on top of the palm leaves using mustard yellow yarn. Using yarn leftovers in different colors, you can make a few stitches here and there to make the print your very own.

Sew tiny buttons to rows 18, 14, 10 and 6 of the shirt. Use corresponding loops on the opposite side of the shirt as buttonholes.

RADIO

SPEAKER
* *in graphite yarn*

Rnd 1: start 6 sc in a magic ring [6]
Rnd 2: inc in all 6 st [12]
Fasten off and weave in the yarn end on the wrong side of your work.

FRONT DECK
* *in mauve yarn*

Ch 9. Stitches are worked around both sides of the foundation chain.
Rnd 1: start in second ch from hook, inc in next ch, sc in next 6 ch, 4 sc in next ch. Continue on the other side of the foundation chain, sc in next 6 ch, inc in next ch [20]
Rnd 2: (sc in next st, inc in next st, sc in next 6 st, inc in next st, sc in next st) repeat 2 times [24]
Rnd 3: (sc in next st, inc in next 2 st, sc in next 6 st, inc in next 2 st, sc in next st) repeat 2 times [32]
Rnd 4: (sc in next 2 st, inc in next 2 st, sc in next 8 st, inc in next 2 st, sc in next 2 st) repeat 2 times [40]
Fasten off and weave in the yarn end on the wrong side of your work.

Sew the speaker on the left side of the front deck using a single strand of graphite yarn. Embroider the tuning panel by making 2-3 stitches (approximately 3 stitches long) using a strand of off-white yarn.

Sew a few tiny buttons on the right bottom side of the

24   25   26   27

front deck. Alternatively, you can use small beads or embroider French knots.

Cut two pieces of plastic or cardboard matching the size of the front deck. These will be used to reinforce the radio later.

RADIO CASE
in mauve yarn

Rnd 1 – 4: repeat the instructions for Rnd 1-4 of the front deck.

Rnd 5: BLO sc in all 40 st [40]

Rnd 6 – 7: sc in all 40 st [40]

Don't fasten off, in the next round we're joining the radio case and the front deck together (picture 24).

Put one of the plastic or cardboard pieces you cut earlier inside the case and cover it with fiberfill. Put the second piece of plastic or cardboard on top of it (picture 24) and cover it with the front deck. Align the parts nicely and join them in the next round by working through both the front deck and the radio case.

Rnd 8: slst in all 40 st through both layers [40] (picture 26)

If needed, add some more fiberfill between the plastic or cardboard pieces before closing the seam. Fasten off and weave in the yarn end.

HANDLE
in mauve yarn

Leave a long starting yarn tail.

Ch 11. Crochet in rows.

Row 1: start in second ch from hook, slst in all 10 ch, ch 1, turn [10]

Row 2: slst in all 10 st [10]

Fasten off, leaving a long tail for sewing. Sew the handle on top of the radio, with 6 stitches between the ends. Weave in the yarn ends.

FINISHING THE RADIO

Make a little antenna out of a piece of crafting wire (see Mom's hairpin instruction, p. 31). Insert it in the top part of the radio and glue it in place (picture 27).

OMA

Oma is a professional skateboarder and a loving grandmother to Lula and Bo. Her spirit is still young and she firmly believes in CAN DO. She runs her female power club at Dad's coffee shop every Wednesday night.

SKILL LEVEL

✳ ✳

SIZE

9" / 22.5 cm tall when made with the indicated yarn.

MATERIALS

- Fingering weight yarn in:
  • black
  • nude
  • jeans blue
  • off-white
  • lavender
  • fuchsia (leftover)
  • gray (leftover)
  • pink (leftover)
- Scraps of graphite, lilac, lime, light brown, white and pink yarn or embroidery thread for the embroidery
- 7 steel / 1.5 mm crochet hook
- Sewing needle
- Yarn needle
- Pins
- 2 flat buttons (diameter 0.5" / 1.4 cm) to strengthen the feet
- 4 tiny buttons (diameter 0.3" / 8 mm) for the skateboard wheels
- Approx. 7.8" / 20 cm of black crafting wire to make the glasses
- A piece of plastic or cardboard to reinforce the skateboard
- Stitch markers
- Fiberfill for stuffing

Scan or visit
www.amigurumi.com/3906
to share pictures and find inspiration.

LEG

✳ *make 2, start in black yarn*

> **Note:** We start by crocheting the legs and trouser legs separately. We continue by attaching the trouser legs directly to the legs, then join the trouser legs together to create the body.

Rnd 1: start 6 sc in a magic ring [6]
Rnd 2: inc in all 6 st [12]
Rnd 3: (sc in next st, inc in next st) repeat 6 times [18]
Rnd 4: BLO sc in all 18 st [18]
Rnd 5: sc in all 18 st [18]

> **Note:** Insert a flat button inside the foot at this point. It's important to keep the soles flat as we want them to have the same shape as cute little hooves.

Rnd 6: (dec, sc in next st) repeat 6 times [12]
Change to nude yarn.
Rnd 7 – 36: sc in all 12 st [12]
Stuff the leg firmly with fiberfill and continue stuffing as you go.
Rnd 37: (sc in next 3 st, inc in next st) repeat 3 times [15]
Rnd 38: sc in next 2 st, (inc in next st, sc in next 4 st) repeat 2 times, inc in next st, sc in next 2 st [18]
Rnd 39: (sc in next 5 st, inc in next st) repeat 3 times [21]
Rnd 40: sc in next 3 st, (inc in next st, sc in next 6 st) repeat 2 times, inc in next st, sc in next 3 st [24]
Rnd 41: (sc in next 7 st, inc in next st) repeat 3 times [27]
Rnd 42: sc in next 4 st, (inc in next st, sc in next 8 st) repeat 2 times, inc in next st, sc in next 4 st [30]
Fasten off and weave in the yarn end. Make sure the leg is stuffed very firmly and evenly. Set the legs aside and make the trouser legs.

TROUSER LEG

✳ *make 2, in jeans blue yarn*

Leave a very long starting yarn tail. You're going to need it to work another round around the bottom of the trouser leg later. Ch 42 and join with a slst to make a circle. Make sure the chain isn't twisted.
Rnd 1: sc in all 42 ch [42]

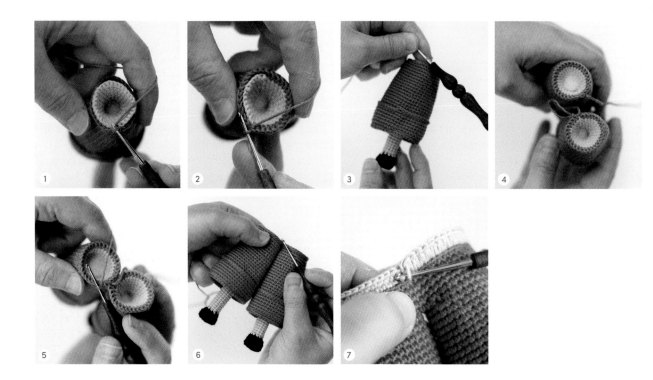

Rnd 2 – 7: sc in all 42 st [42]

Don't fasten off. Go back to round 1 and, using the yarn tail you left at the beginning, work slst around the bottom of the trouser leg. Fasten off and weave in the yarn end on the wrong side of your work. Continue working on round 7.

Rnd 8: FLO slst in all 42 st [42] This will create a decorative seam on the trouser leg.

Rnd 9: work this round in the remaining back loops of Rnd 7: sc in next 6 st, (dec, sc in next 12 st) repeat 2 times, dec, sc in next 6 st [39]

Rnd 10 – 13: sc in all 39 st [39]

Rnd 14: (sc in next 11 st, dec) repeat 3 times [36]

Rnd 15 – 18: sc in all 36 st [36]

Rnd 19: sc in next 5 st, (dec, sc in next 10 st) repeat 2 times, dec, sc in next 5 st [33]

Rnd 20 – 23: sc in all 33 st [33]

Rnd 24: (sc in next 9 st, dec) repeat 3 times [30]

Rnd 25: sc in all 30 st [30]

Crochet an additional 3-4 sc to move the beginning of the round to the side of the trouser leg and mark the last stitch you made, this is the new beginning of the round. Position the trouser leg over the leg and align the edges (picture 1). In the next round, we'll join the leg and the trouser leg together.

Rnd 26: sc in all 30 st through both layers [30] (pictures 2-3)

Fasten off on the first leg, leaving a yarn tail. Join the second leg and trouser leg in the same way, but don't fasten off (picture 4). In the next round, we'll join both trouser legs together and start crocheting the body.

BODY
* continue in nude yarn

Rnd 1: sc in a st on the first trouser leg to join (pictures 5-6), sc in next 29 st on the first trouser leg, sc in all 30 st on the second trouser leg [60]

Crochet an additional 15 sc to move the beginning of the round to the side of the body and mark the last stitch you made, this is the new beginning of the round.

Rnd 2 – 4: sc in all 60 st [60]

Use the yarn tail left on the first leg to sew the gap

between the legs closed.

Rnd 5: sc in next 4 st, (dec, sc in next 8 st) repeat 5 times, dec, sc in next 4 st [54]

Change to gray yarn.

Rnd 6: BLO sc in all 54 st [54]

Rnd 7: sc in all 54 st [54]

Rnd 8: spike st in all 54 st of Rnd 6 [54] (picture 7)

This creates the ribbing of Oma's sweater. Change to off-white yarn.

Rnd 9: BLO sc in all 54 st [54]

Rnd 10: (sc in next 2 st, inc in next st) repeat 18 times [72]

Rnd 11 – 15: sc in all 72 st [72]

Rnd 16: sc in next 11 st, (dec, sc in next 22 st) repeat 2 times, dec, sc in next 11 st [69]

Rnd 17: (sc in next 21 st, dec) repeat 3 times [66]

Rnd 18: sc in next 10 st, (dec, sc in next 20 st) repeat 2 times, dec, sc in next 10 st [63]

Rnd 19: (sc in next 19 st, dec) repeat 3 times [60]

Rnd 20: sc in next 9 st, (dec, sc in next 18 st) repeat 2 times, dec, sc in next 9 st [57]

Rnd 21: (sc in next 17 st, dec) repeat 3 times [54]

Rnd 22: sc in next 8 st, (dec, sc in next 16 st) repeat 2 times, dec, sc in next 8 st [51]

Rnd 23: (sc in next 15 st, dec) repeat 3 times [48]

Rnd 24: sc in all 48 st [48]

Rnd 25: sc in next 7 st, (dec, sc in next 14 st) repeat 2 times, dec, sc in next 7 st [45]

Rnd 26: sc in all 45 st [45]

Rnd 27: (sc in next 13 st, dec) repeat 3 times [42]

Rnd 28: sc in all 42 st [42]

Crochet an additional 4-5 sc to move the beginning of the round to the side of the body and mark the last stitch you made, this is the new beginning of the round. Change to black yarn.

Rnd 29: sc in all 42 st [42]

Change to nude yarn.

Rnd 30: BLO (sc in next 5 st, dec) repeat 6 times [36]

Rnd 31: sc in next 5 st, (dec, sc in next 10 st) repeat 2 times, dec, sc in next 5 st [33]

Rnd 32: (sc in next 9 st, dec) repeat 3 times [30]

Rnd 33: sc in next 4 st, (dec, sc in next 8 st) repeat 2 times, dec, sc in next 4 st [27]

Rnd 34: (sc in next 7 st, dec) repeat 3 times [24]

Fasten off, leaving a long tail for sewing. Stuff the body very firmly with fiberfill.

HEAD

❋ in nude yarn

Rnd 1: start 6 sc in a magic ring [6]

Rnd 2: inc in all 6 st [12]

Rnd 3: (sc in next st, inc in next st) repeat 6 times [18]

Rnd 4: sc in next st, (inc in next st, sc in next 2 st) repeat 5 times, inc in next st, sc in next st [24]

Rnd 5: (sc in next 3 st, inc in next st) repeat 6 times [30]

Rnd 6: sc in next 2 st, (inc in next st, sc in next 4 st) repeat 5 times, inc in next st, sc in next 2 st [36]

Rnd 7: (sc in next 5 st, inc in next st) repeat 6 times [42]

Rnd 8: sc in next 3 st, (inc in next st, sc in next 6 st) repeat 5 times, inc in next st, sc in next 3 st [48]

Rnd 9: (sc in next 7 st, inc in next st) repeat 6 times [54]

Rnd 10: sc in next 4 st, (inc in next st, sc in next 8 st) repeat 5 times, inc in next st, sc in next 4 st [60]

Rnd 11: (sc in next 9 st, inc in next st) repeat 6 times [66]

Rnd 12 – 25: sc in all 66 st [66]

Rnd 26: (sc in next 9 st, dec) repeat 6 times [60]

Rnd 27: sc in next 4 st, (dec, sc in next 8 st) repeat 5 times, dec, sc in next 4 st [54]

Rnd 28: (sc in next 7 st, dec) repeat 6 times [48]

Stuff the head with fiberfill and continue stuffing as you go.

Rnd 29: sc in next 3 st, (dec, sc in next 6 st) repeat 5 times, dec, sc in next 3 st [42]

Rnd 30: (sc in next 5 st, dec) repeat 6 times [36]

Rnd 31: sc in next 2 st, (dec, sc in next 4 st) repeat 5 times, dec, sc in next 2 st [30]

Rnd 32: (sc in next 3 st, dec) repeat 6 times [24]

Rnd 33: work this round in BLO, sc in next st, (dec, sc in next 2 st) repeat 5 times, dec, sc in next st [18]

Finish stuffing the head very firmly.

Rnd 34: (dec, sc in next st) repeat 6 times [12]

Rnd 35: dec 6 times [6]

Fasten off, leaving a yarn tail. Using a yarn needle, weave the yarn tail through the front loop of each remaining stitch and pull it tight to close. Weave in the yarn end. Sew the head and the body together using the leftover front loops of round 32 of the head.

ARM
* *make 2, start in nude yarn*

Rnd 1: start 6 sc in a magic ring [6]
Rnd 2: (sc in next st, inc in next st) repeat 3 times [9]
Rnd 3: sc in all 9 st [9]
Rnd 4: sc in next 4 st, 5-dc-bobble in next st, sc in next 4 st [9]
Rnd 5 – 9: sc in all 9 st [9]
Change to black yarn.

> **Note:** *Make sure the color change is at the inside of the arm, add a few sc or undo a few to get to this point.*

Rnd 10: BLO sc in all 9 st [9]
Stuff the hand with fiberfill and continue stuffing as you go.
Rnd 11: spike st in all 9 st [9]
Rnd 12: BLO inc in all 9 st [18]
Rnd 13: sc in next st, (inc in next st, sc in next 2 st) repeat 5 times, inc in next st, sc in next st [24]
Rnd 14: (sc in next 3 st, inc in next st) repeat 6 times [30]
Rnd 15: sc in next 2 st, (inc in next st, sc in next 4 st) repeat 5 times, inc in next st, sc in next 2 st [36]
Rnd 16 – 17: sc in all 36 st [36]
Rnd 18: sc in next 5 st, (dec, sc in next 10 st) repeat 2 times, dec, sc in next 5 st [33]
Rnd 19: sc in all 33 st [33]
Rnd 20: (sc in next 9 st, dec) repeat 3 times [30]
Rnd 21: sc in all 30 st [30]
Rnd 22: sc in next 4 st, (dec, sc in next 8 st) repeat 2 times, dec, sc in next 4 st [27]
Rnd 23: sc in all 27 st [27]
Rnd 24: (sc in next 7 st, dec) repeat 3 times [24]
Rnd 25: sc in all 24 st [24]
Rnd 26: sc in next 3 st, (dec, sc in next 6 st) repeat 2 times, dec, sc in next 3 st [21]
Rnd 27 – 28: sc in all 21 st [21]
Rnd 29: (sc in next 5 st, dec) repeat 3 times [18]
Rnd 30 – 31: sc in all 18 st [18]
Rnd 32: sc in next 2 st, (dec, sc in next 4 st) repeat 2 times, dec, sc in next 2 st [15]
Rnd 33: sc in all 15 st [15]
Rnd 34: (sc in next 3 st, dec) repeat 3 times [12]
Rnd 35: sc in all 12 st [12]

Stuff only the lower half of the arms with fiberfill, so the arms don't stick out too much after sewing. Flatten the arm and work the next round through both layers to close. Make a couple of additional sc or undo a few to get to the opposite side of the thumb.
Rnd 36: sc in all 6 st [6]
Fasten off, leaving a long tail for sewing. Sew the arms to the sides of the body, right underneath round 29 (the round worked in black).

HAIR
* *in lavender yarn*

> **Note:** *Oma's hair is made like a beanie (similar to Bo's hair), with the front side shorter than the back.*

Leave a long starting yarn tail. Ch 23. Crochet in rows.
Row 1: start in second ch from hook, slst in next 4 ch, sc in next 4 ch, hdc in next 14 ch, ch 1, turn [22]
Row 2: hdc in next st, BLO hdc in next 13 st, BLO sc in next 4 st, BLO slst in next 3 st, slst in next st, ch 1, turn [22]
Row 3: slst in next st, BLO slst in next 3 st, BLO sc in next 4 st, BLO hdc in next 13 st, hdc in next st, ch 1, turn [22]
Row 4 – 8: repeat rows 2 and 3 alternately [22]
Row 9: slst in next st, BLO slst in next 3 st, BLO sc in next 4 st, BLO hdc in next 5 st, hdc in next st, ch 1, turn [14]
Leave the remaining stitches unworked.
Row 10: hdc in next st, BLO hdc in next 5 st, BLO sc in next 4 st, BLO slst in next 3 st, slst in next st, ch 1, turn [14]
Row 11 – 32: repeat rows 9 and 10 alternately [14]
Row 33: slst in next st, BLO slst in next 3 st, BLO sc in next 4 st, BLO hdc in next 5 st, hdc in next st, ch 9, turn [14 + 9 ch]
Row 34: start in second ch from hook, hdc in next 8 ch, hdc in next st, BLO hdc in next 5 st, BLO sc in next 4 st, BLO slst in next 3 st, slst in next st, ch 1, turn [22]
Row 35 – 46: repeat rows 2 and 3 alternately [22]
Don't fasten off, but continue crocheting the top of the hair. Continue crocheting in rounds.
Rnd 1: join the end of row 46 with the beginning of row 1 with a slst. Work sc in all row-ends around the crown [24] (picture 8).

> **Note:** *If you have one stitch more or less in this round, make an extra decrease or skip one just to make it easier to work the last rounds. It's all good*

as long as it looks neat.

Rnd 2: (sc in next st, dec) repeat 8 times [16]

Rnd 3: dec 8 times [8]

Fasten off, leaving a long yarn tail. Using a yarn needle, weave the yarn tail through the front loop of each remaining stitch and pull it tight to close. Weave in the yarn end on the wrong side of your work (picture 9). Using the starting yarn tail, sew both sides of the hair together (picture 10). Position the hair on the head. Smoothen the hair to make sure it enwraps the head nicely. Secure it with pins. Split a piece of lavender yarn into strands and take one or two strands on a yarn needle to sew the hair to the head. Don't sew the lower right part of the hair to the head, so it can be turned up for a more playful look.

EAR

✳ *make 2, in nude yarn*

Leave a long starting yarn tail.

Rnd 1: start 5 sc in a magic ring [5]

Pull the magic ring tightly closed and fasten off, leaving a tail for sewing. Sew the ears to the head, in the corners of the hair. Weave in the yarn ends.

TURTLENECK

✳ *in black yarn*

Ch 17. Crochet in rows.

Row 1: start in second ch from hook, sc in next 8 ch, hdc in next 8 ch, ch 1, turn [16]

Row 2: hdc in next st, BLO hdc in next 7 st, BLO sc in next 7 st, sc in next st, ch 1, turn [16]

Row 3: sc in next st, BLO sc in next 7 st, BLO hdc in next 7 st, hdc in next st, ch 1, turn [16]

Row 4 – 38: repeat row 2 and 3 alternately [16]

> **Note:** The turtleneck shouldn't be too large, the lower part should have the same length as round 29 of the body. Try it on as you go and adjust the size according to how firmly you crochet by making 1-2 rows more or less.

Fasten off, leaving a long tail for sewing. Pin the turtleneck to round 29 of the body (the round made in black).

Split a piece of black yarn into strands and take one or two strands on a yarn needle to sew the lower part of the turtleneck to the leftover front loops of round 29. Using the yarn tail at the end, sew the short sides of the turtleneck together and fold the turtleneck over (picture 11).

FLYING UNICORN PRINT

HEAD

✳ *in pink yarn*

Rnd 1: start 6 sc in a magic ring [6]

Rnd 2: inc in all 6 st [12]

Rnd 3: (inc in next st, sc in next st) repeat 6 times [18]

Fasten off and weave in the yarn end on the wrong side of your work.

BODY
* in pink yarn

Ch 5. Stitches are worked around both sides of the foundation chain.
Rnd 1: start in second ch from hook, sc in next 3 ch, 4 sc in next ch. Continue on the other side of the foundation chain, sc in next 2 ch, 3 sc in next ch [12]
Rnd 2: inc in next st, sc in next 2 st, inc in next 4 st, sc in next 2 st, inc in next 3 st [20]
Fasten off and weave in the yarn end on the wrong side of your work.
Pin the head and the body of the unicorn in the center of Oma's sweater. Split a piece of pink yarn into strands and thread one or two strands on a yarn needle to sew the parts into place. Embroider four French knots underneath the body and two more on top of the head for the legs and ears. Using lime embroidery thread, make four

Lazy Daisy stitches for the wings. Using lilac embroidery thread, embroider a few straight stitches for the horn. Don't forget to give the unicorn a funny face (picture 12).

FINISHING TOUCHES

• Embroider the facial features. A water-soluble marker or sewing pins may come in handy to mark out the position of the eyes, eyebrows, nose and cheeks first. The eyes are embroidered using one or two strands of graphite yarn or black embroidery thread. Position the eyes 3 rounds below the fringe, with an inter-space of approximately 16-17 stitches. Embroider the eyebrows using light brown yarn. Embroider the nose over 1 stitch in between the eyes using a single strand of nude yarn. Highlight the bottom of the nose using graphite yarn or black embroidery thread. Embroider the cheeks underneath the eyes using pink embroidery thread.
• Using a single strand of black yarn, make two long stitches (starting from the bottom of the sweater and ending underneath the turtleneck) to imitate the seams.
• To make the glasses, wrap a piece of crafting wire around a round object. Skip a section about the distance between the eyes, then wrap the wire around the round object again, and cut off the excess wire. There should be approximately 1.2" / 3 cm left on the ends for the earpieces. Insert the earpieces into the head at 3-4 stitches from each eye.
• Use some leftover crafting wire to make hoop earrings.

SKATEBOARD

DECK
* make 2, in fuchsia yarn

Ch 28. Stitches are worked around both sides of the foundation chain.
Rnd 1: start in second ch from hook, sc in next 26 ch, 3 sc in next ch. Continue on the other side of the foundation chain, sc in next 25 ch, inc in next ch [56]
Rnd 2: inc in next st, sc in next 25 st, inc in next 3 st,

sc in next 25 st, inc in next 2 st [62]

Rnd 3: sc in next st, inc in next st, (sc in next st, inc in next st) repeat 3 times, sc in next 25 st, (sc in next st, inc in next st) repeat 2 times [68]

Rnd 4: sc in next st, inc in next st, sc in next 25 st, (sc in next 2 st, inc in next st) repeat 3 times, sc in next 25 st, (sc in next 2 st, inc in next st) repeat 2 times, sc in next st [74]

Rnd 5: sc in next 3 st, inc in next st, (sc in next 3 st, inc in next st) repeat 3 times, sc in next 25 st, (sc in next 3 st, inc in next st) repeat 2 times [80]

Rnd 6: sc in next 2 st, inc in next st, sc in next 25 st, (sc in next 4 st, inc in next st) repeat 3 times, sc in next 25 st, (sc in next 4 st, inc in next st) repeat 2 times, sc in next 2 st [86]

Fasten off on the first deck and weave in the yarn end on the wrong side of your work. Don't fasten off on the second deck.

Cut two pieces of plastic or cardboard in an oval shape matching the shape of the deck. These will be used to reinforce the skateboard. Put the decks on top of each other, with the wrong sides facing and the plastic or cardboard pieces between them. Work the next round through both decks to join them together.

Rnd 7: slst in all 86 st around [86] (pictures 13-14)

Fasten off and weave in the yarn end. Bend the edges of the deck to give it a real skateboard shape.

TRUCK

* make 2, in fuchsia yarn

Rnd 1: start 7 sc in a magic ring [7]

Rnd 2 – 12: sc in all 7 st [7]

> **Note:** Make sure that the truck has the same length as the width of the deck. If needed, crochet a round more or less than the pattern calls for.

Fasten off, leaving a yarn tail. Using a yarn needle, weave the yarn tail through the front loop of each remaining stitch and pull it tight to close. Weave in the yarn end. Sew the trucks to the bottom of the deck. If you have a glue gun, don't hesitate to use it. Sew flat buttons on each side of both trucks using white embroidery thread to mimic the wheels (picture 15).

GARY

Gary is Lula's neighbor. He's the partner of Hadi and the proud father of their daughter Maja and their dog Yoyo. He used to be a sailor, but now that he's retired, he's dedicated himself to growing his own organic produce in the garden. You can always ask him for some great eco-friendly tips.

SKILL LEVEL

* *

SIZE

8.5" / 21.5 cm tall when made with the indicated yarn.

MATERIALS

- Fingering weight yarn in:
  • nude
  • red
  • graphite
  • off-white
  • mauve
  • deep blue
  • jeans blue
- Scraps of yarn or embroidery thread in different colors for the embroidery
- 7 and 4 steel / 1.5 and 1.75 mm crochet hooks
- Sewing needle
- Yarn needle
- Pins
- 4 tiny buttons (diameter 1/16" / 2 mm) for the shirt and 1 tiny bead for the earring
- A stainless hook (like a small poster hanger) for Gary's left hand
- Stitch markers
- Fiberfill for stuffing

Scan or visit
www.amigurumi.com/3907
to share pictures and find inspiration.

Note: *All parts are worked with a 7 steel / 1.5 mm crochet hook, except for the beard and moustache, jeans and shirt (these are worked with a 4 steel / 1.75 mm crochet hook).*

LEG
* *make 2, start in graphite yarn*

Ch 7. Stitches are worked around both sides of the foundation chain.
Rnd 1: start in second ch from hook, sc in next 5 ch, 4 sc in next ch. Continue on the opposite side of the foundation chain, sc in next 4 ch, 3 sc in next ch [16]
Rnd 2: (inc in next st, sc in next 4 st) repeat 2 times, inc in next 3 st [24]
Rnd 3: BLO sc in all 24 st [24]
Rnd 4: sc in all 24 st [24]
Rnd 5: sc in next 6 st, dec 6 times, sc in next 6 st [18]
Rnd 6: sc in next 6 st, dec 3 times, sc in next 6 st [15]
Change to nude yarn.
Rnd 7 – 24: sc in all 15 st [15]
Change to red yarn. Stuff the leg firmly with fiberfill and continue stuffing as you go.
Rnd 25: BLO sc in all 15 st [15]
Rnd 26: spike st in all 15 st [15]
Rnd 27: BLO sc in all 15 st [15]
Rnd 28: sc in all 15 st [15]
Fasten off on the first leg and weave in the yarn end. Don't fasten off on the second leg. In the next round, we'll join both legs together and start crocheting the body.

BODY
* *continue working in red yarn*

Rnd 1: sc in next 5 st on the second leg, ch 9 and join to the first leg with a sc (make sure the feet point forward), sc in next 14 st on the first leg, sc in next 9 ch, sc in next 10 st on the second leg [48]
Rnd 2: (sc in next 7 st, inc in next st) repeat 6 times [54]
Rnd 3: sc in next 4 st, (inc in next st, sc in next 8 st) repeat 5 times, inc in next st, sc in next 4 st [60]
Rnd 4: (sc in next 9 st, inc in next st) repeat 6 times [66]

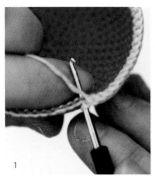

Rnd 5 – 7: sc in all 66 st [66]
Rnd 8: BLO sc in all 66 st [66]
Rnd 9: spike st in all 66 st [66]
Change to nude yarn.
Rnd 10: BLO sc in all 66 st [66]
Rnd 11 – 28: sc in all 66 st [66]
Rnd 29: sc in next 10 st, (dec, sc in next 20 st) repeat 2 times, dec, sc in next 10 st [63]
Rnd 30: (sc in next 19 st, dec) repeat 3 times [60]
Stuff the body with fiberfill and continue stuffing as you go.
Rnd 31: sc in next 9 st, (dec, sc in next 18 st) repeat 2 times, dec, sc in next 9 st [57]
Rnd 32: (sc in next 17 st, dec) repeat 3 times [54]
Rnd 33: sc in next 8 st, (dec, sc in next 16 st) repeat 2 times, dec, sc in next 8 st [51]
Rnd 34: (sc in next 15 st, dec) repeat 3 times [48]
Rnd 35: sc in next 7 st, (dec, sc in next 14 st) repeat 2 times, dec, sc in next 7 st [45]
Rnd 36: (sc in next 13 st, dec) repeat 3 times [42]
Rnd 37: sc in next 6 st, (dec, sc in next 12 st) repeat 2 times, dec, sc in next 6 st [39]
Rnd 38: (sc in next 11 st, dec) repeat 3 times [36]
Fasten off, leaving a long tail for sewing.

> **Note:** *Make sure the body is stuffed firmly. If it's too soft, it might be damaged in the assembly and embroidery process.*

HEAD

* *start in deep blue yarn*

Rnd 1: start 6 sc in a magic ring [6]
Rnd 2: inc in all 6 st [12]
Rnd 3: (sc in next st, inc in next st) repeat 6 times [18]
Rnd 4: sc in next st, (inc in next st, sc in next 2 st) repeat 5 times, inc in next st, sc in next st [24]
Rnd 5: (sc in next 3 st, inc in next st) repeat 6 times [30]
Rnd 6: sc in next 2 st, (inc in next st, sc in next 4 st) repeat 5 times, inc in next st, sc in next 2 st [36]
Rnd 7: (sc in next 5 st, inc in next st) repeat 6 times [42]
Rnd 8: sc in next 3 st, (inc in next st, sc in next 6 st) repeat 5 times, inc in next st, sc in next 3 st [48]
Rnd 9: (sc in next 7 st, inc in next st) repeat 6 times [54]
Rnd 10: sc in next 4 st, (inc in next st, sc in next 8 st) repeat 5 times, inc in next st, sc in next 4 st [60]
Rnd 11 – 13: sc in all 60 st [60]
Rnd 14: (sc in next 9 st, inc in next st) repeat 6 times [66]
Change to nude yarn, but don't fasten off the deep blue yarn just yet. Leave it hanging on the outside of your work.
Rnd 15: BLO slst in all 66 st [66]
Work the next round in the back loops of both round 14 and round 15 (pictures 1-2).
Rnd 16: sc in all 66 st [66]
Rnd 17: (sc in next 10 st, inc in next st) repeat 6 times [72]
Rnd 18 – 30: sc in all 72 st [72]
Rnd 31: sc in next 5 st, (dec, sc in next 10 st) repeat 5 times, dec, sc in next 5 st [66]
Do not fasten off. Take a break and return to round 14. Hold the head with the opening towards you. Take the

deep blue yarn on the outside of your work on your crochet hook and start in the first unworked front loop of round 14 where the yarn appears.

Rnd 1: FLO sc in all 66 st [66]
Rnd 2 – 3: (FPdc in next st, BPdc in next st) repeat 33 times [66] (pictures 3-4)
Fasten off and weave in the yarn end. Return to the head.
Rnd 32: (sc in next 9 st, dec) repeat 6 times [60]
Rnd 33: sc in next 4 st, (dec, sc in next 8 st) repeat 5 times, dec, sc in next 4 st [54]
Rnd 34: (sc in next 7 st, dec) repeat 6 times [48]
Stuff the head with fiberfill and continue stuffing as you go.
Rnd 35: sc in next 3 st, (dec, sc in next 6 st) repeat 5 times, dec, sc in next 3 st [42]
Rnd 36: (sc in next 5 st, dec) repeat 6 times [36]
Rnd 37: work this round in BLO, sc in next 2 st, (dec, sc in next 4 st) repeat 5 times, dec, sc in next 2 st [30]
Rnd 38: (sc in next 3 st, dec) repeat 6 times [24]
Rnd 39: sc in next st, (dec, sc in next 2 st) repeat 5 times, dec, sc in next st [18]
Finish stuffing the head very firmly.
Rnd 40: (dec, sc in next st) repeat 6 times [12]
Rnd 41: dec 6 times [6]
Fasten off, leaving a yarn tail. Using a yarn needle, weave the yarn tail through the front loop of each remaining stitch and pull it tight to close. Weave in the yarn end. Sew the head to the body using the leftover front loops of round 36 of the head.

RIGHT ARM
* in nude yarn

Rnd 1: start 5 sc in a magic ring [5]
Rnd 2: inc in all 5 st [10]
Rnd 3: sc in all 10 st [10]
Rnd 4: sc in next 4 st, 5-dc-bobble in next st, sc in next 5 st [10]
Rnd 5 – 31: sc in all 10 st [10]
Stuff only the lower half of the arm with fiberfill, so it doesn't stick out too much after sewing. Flatten the arm and work the next round through both layers to close. Make a couple of additional sc or undo a few to

get to the opposite side of the thumb.
Rnd 32: sc in all 5 st [5]
Fasten off, leaving a long tail for sewing.

LEFT ARM
* start in graphite yarn

Note: The left and right arm are worked differently (Gary has a hook instead of his left hand). If you feel too bad about Gary's loss, make the left arm the same way as the right arm. If you think scars are a man's ornaments, follow the separate instructions below.

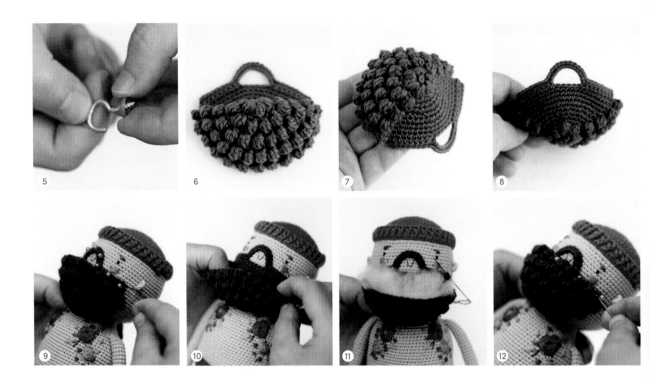

Rnd 1: start 5 sc in a magic ring [5]
Don't pull the magic ring too tight, but leave a small
hole to insert the hook later.
Rnd 2: inc in all 5 st [10]
Rnd 3 – 5: sc in all 10 st [10]
Insert the hook into the magic ring and secure it with a
plastic washer on the inside, the same way you would
do when using safety eyes (picture 5). If a regular safe-
ty eye washer doesn't match the hook you have, don't
hesitate to use a glue gun. A pea-sized drop of hot glue
on the inside of the arm is enough to secure the hook.
Rnd 6: BLO sc in all 10 st [10]
Rnd 7: spike st in all 10 st [10]
Change to nude yarn.

> **Note:** *Make sure the color change is at the inside
> of the arm, add a few sc or undo a few to get to this
> point.*

Rnd 8: BLO sc in all 10 st [10]
Rnd 9 – 27: sc in all 10 st [10]
Stuff only the lower half of the arm with fiberfill, so it
doesn't stick out too much after sewing. Flatten the arm
and work the next round through both layers to close.

Rnd 28: sc in all 5 st [5]
Fasten off, leaving a long tail for sewing. Sew the arms
between rounds 32 and 33 of the body.

BEARD AND MOUSTACHE
* *in graphite yarn, using a 1.75 mm hook*

Rnd 1: start 6 sc in a magic ring [6]
Rnd 2: (5-dc-bobble in next st, ch 1) repeat 6 times [12]
Rnd 3: inc in all 12 st [24]
Rnd 4: (5-dc-bobble in next st, sc in next st) repeat
7 times, sc in next 10 st [24]
Rnd 5: (sc in next st, inc in next st) repeat 12 times [36]
Rnd 6: (5-dc-bobble in next st, sc in next st) repeat
10 times, sc in next 16 st [36]
Rnd 7: sc in next st, (inc in next st, sc in next 2 st) repeat
11 times, inc in next st, sc in next st [48]
Rnd 8: (5-dc-bobble in next st, sc in next st) repeat
13 times, sc in next 22 st [48]
Rnd 9: sc in all 48 st [48]
Rnd 10: (5-dc-bobble in next st, sc in next st) repeat

13 times, sc in next 22 st [48] Leave the remaining stitches unworked.
Continue making the moustache. You're going to work along the smooth side (the last 22 stitches you just made). Continue crocheting in rows.
Row 1: ch 1, turn, sc in next 8 st, slst in next st, ch 10, skip next 4 st, slst in next st, sc in next 8 st, ch 1, turn [18 + 10 ch]
> *Note: When working the moustache in row 2, you insert the hook underneath the chain, not in the individual chain stitches, so the stitches are "wrapping" the chain (see Mom's purse, pictures 10-11, p.30).*
Row 2: sc in next 8 st, skip next st, 16 sc in the ch-10-space, skip next st, sc in next 7 st, slst in next st [32] Fasten off and weave in the yarn end (pictures 6-8).
> *Note: The finished beard should look like a funny grocery bag with one handle.*

FINISHING TOUCHES

- Pin the smooth side of the beard in the middle of the head. The upper edge of the beard should be approximately 8 rounds below the edge of the hat. Give the moustache a nice arched shape and secure it with pins.
- First, embroider the facial features while the beard hasn't been sewn to the head yet.
> *Note: You can save it for later, but we find it more convenient to try everything on at once and embroider the face at this stage, while you can still adjust the position of the beard.*
A water-soluble marker or sewing pins may come in handy to mark out the position of the eyes, mouth, eyebrows and cheeks. The eyes are embroidered using one or two strands of graphite yarn or black embroidery thread. Position them at approximately 5 rounds from the edge of the hat, at 4-5 stitches from each side of the beard and with an interspace of approximately 15-17 stitches. Embroider the cheeks underneath the eyes using pink embroidery thread.
- Second, sew on the top side of the beard. Split a piece of graphite yarn into strands and take two strands on a yarn needle to sew only the top side of the beard

and the moustache in place. Don't touch the rest of the beard just yet (pictures 9-10).
- Put a little bit of stuffing inside the basket-shaped beard and fold the beard closed by pinning the upper edge of the beard on top of the smooth side (pictures 11-12). Use another double strand of graphite yarn to sew the beard neatly closed. The bottom of the beard doesn't need to be sewn to the head.

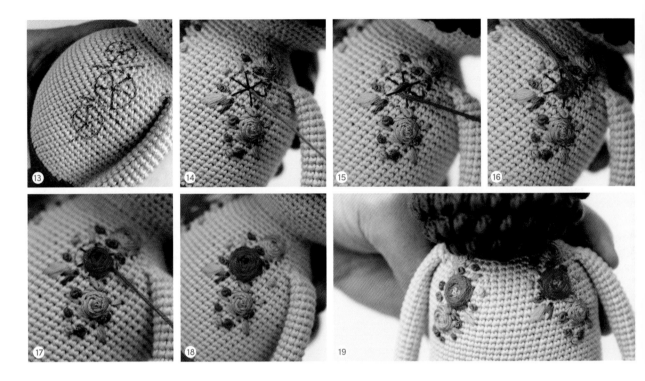

EAR

* make 2, in nude yarn

Leave a long starting yarn tail.
Rnd 1: start 5 sc in a magic ring [5]
Pull the magic ring tightly closed and fasten off, leaving a long tail for sewing. Sew the ears to both sides of the head, approximately 6-7 rounds below the edge of the hat. Weave in the yarn ends. Sew a tiny bead to one of Gary's ears to make an earring.

TATTOOS

Note: *No one (except for Hadi) knows exactly what's underneath Gary's shirt, but as someone might decide to unbutton and peek underneath, we decided to give the guy some tattoos. Tattoos are every hipster vegan's essential attribute after all.*
Draw a few flowers on Gary's chest with a water-soluble marker (picture 13). Use scraps of yarn in different colors or embroidery thread (we used the yarn leftovers from making other characters) to make some straight stitches and French knots. Make sure to split your yarn and use one or two strands for embroidery. To make big flowers (our guess is they're peonies), make 5-6 straight stitches starting at a central point to form a snowflake shape. Then wrap your yarn tail around them the same way as you would do when weaving the bottom of a basket, going over and under the straight stitches. Add a few small French knots in the center (pictures 14-19).

MOM JEANS

* in jeans blue yarn, with a 4 steel / 1.75 mm crochet hook

Note: *Gary's cozy mom jeans are similar to Dad's trousers and Opa's shorts. You start with the upper part and then divide it to make the trouser legs.*
Ch 66 and join with a slst to make a circle. Make sure the chain isn't twisted.

Rnd 1: sc in all 66 ch [66]

>   **Note:** Try it on, the waistband should fit the body nicely. If it's too tight, consider using a bigger hook. If it's too loose, you might want to use a smaller hook.

Rnd 2: (sc in next 10 st, inc in next st) repeat 6 times [72]

Rnd 3 – 16: sc in all 72 st [72]

Flatten your work and divide it into 36 stitches for each trouser leg. Continue working the first trouser leg.

Rnd 17: sc in next 36 st, skip next 36 st [36]

Continue working on these 36 stitches only.

Rnd 18 – 19: sc in all 36 st [36]

Rnd 20: sc in next 5 st, (dec, sc in next 10 st) repeat 2 times, dec, sc in next 5 st [33]

Rnd 21 – 22: sc in all 33 st [33]

Rnd 23: (sc in next 9 st, dec) repeat 3 times [30]

Rnd 24 – 25: sc in all 30 st [30]

Rnd 26: sc in next 4 st, (dec, sc in next 8 st) repeat 2 times, dec, sc in next 4 st [27]

Rnd 27 – 28: sc in all 27 st [27]

Rnd 29: (sc in next 7 st, dec) repeat 3 times [24]

Rnd 30 – 31: sc in all 24 st [24]

Crochet a few additional sc to move the end of the round to the inner side of the trouser leg. Fasten off and weave in the yarn end. Pull up a loop of jeans blue yarn in the next unworked stitch of round 16 of the trousers to make the second trouser leg.

Rnd 17: sc in next 36 st [36]

Rnd 18 – 31: repeat the instructions for the first trouser leg.

Fasten off and weave in the yarn end. Pull up a loop of jeans blue yarn in round 1 of the jeans.

Additional round: sc in all 66 st to strengthen the waistband [66]

Fasten off and weave in the yarn end.

OVERSIZED HIPSTER SHIRT

* start in mauve yarn, with a 4 steel / 1.75 mm crochet hook

>   **Note:** Gary's shirt is similar to Opa's (pictures 20-23 on p.54). Try the shirt on as you go: it should be a little bit tight at the top (so you can see some tattoos) and a bit looser from the chest down (so you're able to button it), but not too loose, as you want a shirt, not a hospital robe. You can use a bigger or smaller hook to tighten or loosen your crochetwork.

Ch 43. Crochet in rows.

Row 1: start in second ch from hook, sc in all 42 ch, ch 2, turn [42]

Change to off-white yarn.

Row 2: hdc in all 42 st, ch 2, turn [42]

Row 3: (hdc in next 5 st, hdc2tog) repeat 6 times, ch 1,

turn [36]

Row 4: sc in all 36 st, ch 2, turn [36]

Check to see if the collar hugs the neck nicely.

Row 5: (hdc in next 6 st, hdc inc in next st, hdc in next 4 st, hdc inc in next st, hdc in next 6 st) repeat 2 times, ch 2, turn [40]

Change to mauve yarn.

Row 6: (hdc in next 6 st, hdc inc in next 2 st, hdc in next 4 st, hdc inc in next 2 st, hdc in next 6 st) repeat 2 times, ch 2, turn [48]

Change to off-white yarn.

Row 7: (hdc in next 6 st, hdc inc in next 2 st, hdc in next 8 st, hdc inc in next 2 st, hdc in next 6 st) repeat 2 times, ch 2, turn [56]

Row 8: (hdc in next 6 st, hdc inc in next 2 st, hdc in next 12 st, hdc inc in next 2 st, hdc in next 6 st) repeat 2 times, ch 2, turn [64]

Row 9: hdc in next 3 st, hdc inc in next 2 st, hdc in next 3 st, ch 8, skip next 10 st (this will be the first armhole), hdc in next 28 st, ch 8, skip next 10 st (this will be the second armhole), hdc in next 3 st, hdc inc in next 2 st, hdc in next 3 st, ch 2, turn [48+16ch]

Change to mauve yarn.

Row 10: hdc in next 10 st, hdc in next 8 ch, hdc in next 3 st, (hdc inc in next st, hdc in next 6 st) repeat 3 times, hdc inc in next st, hdc in next 3 st, hdc in next 8 ch, hdc in next 10 st, ch 2, turn [68]

Change to off-white yarn.

Row 11: hdc in next 8 st, (hdc inc in next st, hdc in next 16 st) repeat 3 times, hdc inc in next st, hdc in next 8 st, ch 2, turn [72]

Row 12 – 13: hdc in all 72 st, ch 2, turn [72]

Change to mauve yarn.

Row 14: hdc in all 72 st, ch 2, turn [72]

Change to off-white yarn.

Row 15 – 17: hdc in all 72 st, ch 2, turn [72]

Change to mauve yarn.

Row 18: hdc in all 72 st, ch 2, turn [72]

Change to off-white yarn.

Row 19 – 21: hdc in all 72 st, ch 2, turn [72]

Change to mauve yarn.

Row 22: hdc in all 72 st, ch 2, turn [72]

Change to off-white yarn.

Row 23: hdc in all 72 st, ch 2, turn [72]

Row 24: hdc in all 72 st [72]

Fasten off and weave in the yarn ends on the wrong side of your work.

SLEEVES

⁎ in off-white yarn

Pull up a loop of off-white yarn at the bottom center of the armhole (picture 23 in Opa's pattern, p. 54).

Rnd 1: sc in next 4 st, sc in the side post of the armhole, sc in next 2 st, hdc in next 6 st, sc in next 2 st, sc in the side post of the armhole, sc in next 4 st [20]

Change to mauve yarn.

Rnd 2: sc in next 7 st, hdc in next 6 st, sc in next 7 st [20]

Change to off-white yarn.

Rnd 3 – 5: hdc in all 20 st [20]

Change to mauve yarn.

Rnd 6: hdc in all 20 st [20]

Change to off-white yarn.

Rnd 7: sc in all 20 st [20]

Rnd 8: slst in all 20 st [20]

Fasten off and weave in the yarn end. Make the second sleeve in the same way. Sew tiny buttons to rows 22, 18, 14 and 10 of the shirt. Use corresponding loops on the opposite side (you can also use the spaces between stitches) of the shirt as buttonholes.

YOYO

Yoyo the Dalmatian is Gary's little helper. His favorite game is chasing the moles to make sure they don't ruin Gary's garden. He loves a nice treat and is not afraid to use his puppy eyes to get them.

SKILL LEVEL

∗

SIZE

5" / 12.5 cm tall when made with the indicated yarn.

MATERIALS

- Fingering weight yarn in:
  • off-white
  • jeans blue
  • graphite
  • gray
- Black embroidery thread
- 7 steel / 1.5 mm crochet hook
- Sewing needle
- Yarn needle
- Pins
- Piece of plastic or cardboard (1.7" x 1.7" / 45 x 45 mm)
- Stitch markers
- Fiberfill for stuffing

 Scan or visit
www.amigurumi.com/3908
to share pictures and find inspiration.

HEAD
∗ *in off-white yarn*

Rnd 1: start 6 sc in a magic ring [6]
Rnd 2: inc in all 6 st [12]
Rnd 3: (sc in next 3 st, inc in next st) repeat 3 times [15]
Rnd 4: sc in next 2 st, (inc in next st, sc in next 4 st) repeat 2 times, inc in next st, sc in next 2 st [18]
Rnd 5 – 6: sc in all 18 st [18]
Rnd 7: inc in next 6 st, sc in next 12 st [24]
Rnd 8: (inc in next st, sc in next st) repeat 6 times, sc in next 12 st [30]
Rnd 9: sc in next st, (inc in next st, sc in next 2 st) repeat 5 times, inc in next st, sc in next 13 st [36]
Stuff the head with fiberfill and continue stuffing as you go.
Rnd 10 – 19: sc in all 36 st [36]
Rnd 20: sc in next 2 st, (dec, sc in next 4 st) repeat 5 times, dec, sc in next 2 st [30]
Rnd 21: (sc in next 3 st, dec) repeat 6 times [24]
Rnd 22: sc in next st, (dec, sc in next 2 st) repeat 5 times, dec, sc in next st [18]
Rnd 23: (sc in next st, dec) repeat 6 times [12]
Finish stuffing the head very firmly.
Rnd 24: dec 6 times [6]
Fasten off, leaving a yarn tail. Using a yarn needle, weave the yarn tail through the front loop of each remaining stitch and pull it tight to close. Weave in the yarn end.

BODY
∗ *start in off-white yarn*

Rnd 1: start 6 sc in a magic ring [6]
Rnd 2: inc in all 6 st [12]
Rnd 3: (sc in next st, inc in next st) repeat 6 times [18]
Rnd 4: sc in next st, (inc in next st, sc in next 2 st) repeat 5 times, inc in next st, sc in next st [24]
Rnd 5: (sc in next 3 st, inc in next st) repeat 6 times [30]
Rnd 6: sc in next 2 st, (inc in next st, sc in next 4 st) repeat 5 times, inc in next st, sc in next 2 st [36]
Rnd 7: (sc in next 5 st, inc in next st) repeat 6 times [42]
Rnd 8: sc in next 3 st, (inc in next st, sc in next 6 st) repeat

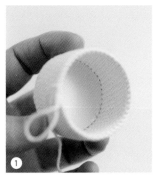

5 times, inc in next st, sc in next 3 st [48]

Rnd 9: BLO sc in all 48 st [48]

Cut a round shape out of a piece of plastic or cardboard. Make it a tiny bit smaller than the bottom of the body you've just crocheted.

> **Note:** It's important to strengthen this part to prevent it from turning into a round shape while stuffing. The bottom needs to be flat if you want the dog to sit instead of roll to one side.

Rnd 10 – 20: sc in all 48 st [48]

Put the plastic or cardboard shape inside your crochetwork (picture 1).

Rnd 21: sc in next 7 st, (dec, sc in next 14 st) repeat 2 times, dec, sc in next 7 st [45]

Rnd 22: (sc in next 13 st, dec) repeat 3 times [42]

Rnd 23: sc in next 6 st, (dec, sc in next 12 st) repeat 2 times, dec, sc in next 6 st [39]

Rnd 24: (sc in next 11 st, dec) repeat 3 times [36]

Change to jeans blue yarn.

Rnd 25: BLO sc in all 36 st [36]

Rnd 26: spike st in all 36 st [36]

Rnd 27: BLO sc in all 36 st [36]

Rnd 28 – 30: sc in all 36 st [36]

Rnd 31: sc in next 5 st, (dec, sc in next 10 st) repeat 2 times, dec, sc in next 5 st [33]

Rnd 32: (sc in next 9 st, dec) repeat 3 times [30]

Rnd 33: sc in next 4 st, (dec, sc in next 8 st) repeat 2 times, dec, sc in next 4 st [27]

Change to off-white yarn.

Rnd 34: (sc in next 7 st, dec) repeat 3 times [24]

Rnd 35: sc in next 3 st, (dec, sc in next 6 st) repeat 2 times, dec, sc in next 3 st [21]

Rnd 36: (sc in next 5 st, dec) repeat 3 times [18]

Slst in next st. Fasten off, leaving a long tail for sewing. Stuff the body very firmly with fiberfill. Pin the body to rounds 13-20 of the head and sew the body in place (picture 2).

HIND LEG
* *make 2, in off-white yarn*

Rnd 1: start 5 sc in a magic ring [5]

Rnd 2: inc in all 5 st [10]

Rnd 3: sc in next 2 st, (3-dc-bobble in next st, sc in next st) repeat 3 times, sc in next 2 st [10]

Rnd 4 – 12: sc in all 10 st [10]

Rnd 13: (sc in next st, inc in next st) repeat 5 times [15]

Rnd 14: sc in next 2 st, (inc in next st, sc in next 4 st) repeat 2 times, inc in next st, sc in next 2 st [18]

Rnd 15: (sc in next 5 st, inc in next st) repeat 3 times [21]

Rnd 16: sc in next 3 st, (inc in next st, sc in next 6 st) repeat 2 times, inc in next st, sc in next 3 st [24]

Stuff the narrow part of the leg (rounds 1-12) firmly with fiberfill.

Rnd 17: (sc in next 7 st, inc in next st) repeat 3 times [27]

Rnd 18: sc in next 4 st, (inc in next st, sc in next 8 st) repeat 2 times, inc in next st, sc in next 4 st [30]

Rnd 19 – 21: sc in all 30 st [30]

Rnd 22: (sc in next 3 st, dec) repeat 6 times [24]

Rnd 23: sc in next st, (dec, sc in next 2 st) repeat 5 times, dec, sc in next st [18]

Rnd 24: (sc in next st, dec) repeat 6 times [12]

Stuff the wide part of the leg (the hip) lightly with fiberfill, you need it to be soft and flat.

Rnd 25: dec 6 times [6] (picture 3)

Fasten off, leaving a yarn tail. Using a yarn needle, weave the yarn tail through the front loop of each remaining stitch and pull it tight to close. Weave in the yarn end. Put the hind legs aside for now.

> **Note:** it's easier to start sewing when all four legs are ready, to balance the construction.

FRONT LEG
✳ *make 2, start in off-white yarn*

Rnd 1: start 6 sc in a magic ring [6]
Rnd 2: (inc in next st, sc in next st) repeat 3 times [9]
Rnd 3: (3-dc-bobble in next st, sc in next st) repeat 3 times, sc in next 3 st [9]
Rnd 4 – 20: sc in all 9 st [9]
Change to jeans blue yarn.
Rnd 21: BLO sc in all 9 st [9]
Rnd 22: spike st in all 9 st [9]
Rnd 23: BLO sc in all 9 st [9]
Rnd 24: sc in all 9 st [9]
Stuff the lower part (rounds 1-17) of the leg with fiberfill. Make a couple of additional sc or undo a few to get to the side of the leg. Flatten the leg and work the next round through both layers to close (picture 4).
Rnd 25: sc in all 4 st [4]
Fasten off, leaving a yarn tail for sewing. Pin the four legs to the body, making sure that the dog's sitting position is balanced. Match the edges of the sleeves on the front legs with the edge of the sweater. The distance between the front legs is approximately 8 stitches. Sew only the hip part of the hind legs to the body. Split the yarn tails into single strands to sew the legs neatly in place.

EAR
✳ *make 2, 1 in gray and 1 in graphite yarn*

Rnd 1: start 6 sc in a magic ring [6]
Rnd 2: (inc in next st, sc in next st) repeat 3 times [9]
Rnd 3: sc in next st, (inc in next st, sc in next 2 st) repeat 2 times, inc in next st, sc in next st [12]
Rnd 4: (sc in next 3 st, inc in next st) repeat 3 times [15]
Rnd 5: sc in next 2 st, (inc in next st, sc in next 4 st) repeat 2 times, inc in next st, sc in next 2 st [18]

  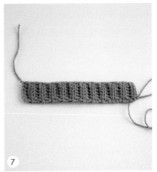 

Rnd 6: (sc in next 5 st, inc in next st) repeat 3 times [21]
Rnd 7: sc in next 3 st, (inc in next st, sc in next 6 st) repeat 2 times, inc in next st, sc in next 3 st [24]
Rnd 8 – 9: sc in all 24 st [24]
The ear doesn't need to be stuffed. Flatten the ear and work the next round through both layers to close.
Rnd 10: sc in all 12 st [12]
Fasten off, leaving a long tail for sewing. Sew the ears to the sides of the head, between rounds 11 and 22, with an interspace of 13 stitches (picture 5).

TAIL
✳ in off-white yarn

Rnd 1: start 4 sc in a magic ring [4]
Rnd 2: (inc in next st, sc in next st) repeat 2 times [6]
Rnd 3 – 5: sc in all 6 st [6]
Rnd 6: inc in next st, sc in next 5 st [7]
Rnd 7 – 8: sc in all 7 st [7]
Rnd 9: inc in next st, sc in next 6 st [8]
Rnd 10 – 11: sc in all 8 st [8]
Rnd 12: inc in next st, sc in next 7 st [9]
Rnd 13: sc in all 9 st [9]
Fasten off, leaving a long tail for sewing. The tail doesn't need to be stuffed. Sew the tail to the back of the body, in the center between rounds 10 and 12 (picture 6).

COLLAR
✳ in jeans blue yarn

Ch 7. Crochet in rows.

Row 1: start in second ch from hook, hdc in all 6 ch, ch 1, turn [6]
Row 2: hdc in next st, BLO hdc in next 4 st, hdc in next st, ch 1, turn [6]
Row 3 – 22: repeat row 2 [6]
Fasten off, leaving a long tail for sewing (picture 7). Wrap the collar around the dog's neck and sew the short ends together. There's no need to attach the collar to the body, as it won't go anywhere (picture 8).

EYE PATCH
✳ in gray yarn

Ch 4. Stitches are worked around both sides of the foundation chain.
Rnd 1: start in second ch from hook, sc in next 2 ch, 3 sc in next ch. Continue on the other side of the foundation chain, sc in next ch, inc in next ch [8]
Rnd 2: inc in next st, sc in next st, inc in next 3 st, sc in next st, inc in next 2 st [14]
Slst in next st. Fasten off and weave in the yarn end on the wrong side of your work. Use a single strand of gray yarn to sew the patch to the left side of the dog's face, between rounds 7 and 12.

BELLY PATCH
✳ in gray yarn

Rnd 1: start 6 sc in a magic ring [6]
Rnd 2: inc in all 6 st [12]
Slst in next st. Fasten off and weave in the yarn end

on the wrong side of your work. Use a single strand of gray yarn to sew the patch to the right side of the belly, 2 rounds below the hem of the sweater.

FINISHING TOUCHES

- Embroider the dog's nose using one or two strands of black yarn, making a few stitches in a triangular shape over round 2 of the muzzle.
- A water-soluble marker or sewing pins may come in handy to mark out the position of the eyes and eyebrows first. Make French knots using one or two strands of black yarn for the eyes. Make 2 straight stitches using 1-2 strands of black yarn to make the eyebrows.
- Embroider a cute little bone print between the front legs on the dog's sweater using off-white yarn. Embroider a horizontal line of 2 stitches long and then embroider 2 French knots on each end.
- Embroider random spots on the dog's body, head and legs using black, graphite and gray yarn. You can make French knots, clusters of backstitches or whatever you like. No mess, no fun, really!

MAJA

Smart and resourceful, Maja is Lula's closest friend. They live right next to each other and grew up playing together in the backyard! Maja likes to build a fortress with all of her books and have teatime with Lula.

SKILL LEVEL

* *

SIZE

8" / 20.5 cm tall when made with the indicated yarn.

MATERIALS

- Fingering weight yarn in
  • light brown
  • graphite
  • grass green
  • salad green
  • mustard yellow (leftover)
  • turquoise (leftover)
  • off-white (leftover)
  • lilac (leftover)
  • mauve (leftover)
- 7 steel / 1.5 mm crochet hook
- Scraps of black and fuchsia yarn or embroidery thread for the embroidery
- Sewing needle
- Yarn needle
- Pins
- 2 flat buttons (diameter 0.5" / 1,4 cm) to strengthen the feet
- Stitch markers
- Fiberfill for stuffing

Scan or visit
www.amigurumi.com/3909
to share pictures and find inspiration.

LEG

* *make 2, start in mustard yellow yarn*

> **Note:** *Maja has fake shorts that are made in the same way as Oma's trousers. We start by crocheting the legs and shorts legs separately. We continue by attaching the shorts legs directly to the legs, then join the shorts legs together to create the body.*

Rnd 1: start 6 sc in a magic ring [6]
Rnd 2: inc in all 6 st [12]
Rnd 3: (sc in next st, inc in next st) repeat 6 times [18]
Rnd 4: BLO sc in all 18 st [18]
Rnd 5: sc in all 18 st [18]

> **Note:** *Insert a flat button inside the foot at this point. It's important to keep the soles flat as we want them to have the same shape as cute little hooves.*

Rnd 6: (dec, sc in next st) repeat 6 times [12]
Change to light brown yarn. Stuff the leg very firmly with fiberfill and continue stuffing as you go.
Rnd 7 – 26: sc in all 12 st [12]
Rnd 27: (sc in next st, inc in next st) repeat 6 times [18]
Rnd 28: sc in next st, (inc in next st, sc in next 2 st) repeat 5 times, inc in next st, sc in next st [24]
Fasten off and weave in the yarn end. Make sure the leg is stuffed very firmly and evenly. Set the legs aside and make the shorts legs.

SHORTS LEG

* *make 2, in salad green yarn*

Leave a very long yarn tail at the beginning. You're going to need it to work another round around the bottom of the shorts leg later.
Ch 24 and join with a slst to make a circle. Make sure the chain isn't twisted.
Rnd 1: sc in all 24 ch [24]
Rnd 2 – 6: sc in all 24 st [24]
Don't fasten off yet. Go back to round 1 and, using the yarn tail you left at the beginning, work slst around the bottom of the shorts leg. Fasten off and weave in the yarn end on the wrong side of your work. Position the shorts leg over the leg and align the edges. In the next round, we'll join the leg and

the shorts leg together.
Rnd 7: sc in all 24 st through both layers [24]
Fasten off, leaving a yarn tail. Join the second leg and shorts leg in the same way, but don't fasten off. In the next round, we'll join both shorts legs together and start crocheting the body.

BODY
❋ *continue in salad green yarn*

Rnd 1: ch 3 and join to the first shorts leg with a sc, sc in next 23 st on the first shorts leg, sc in next 3 ch, sc in all 24 st on the second shorts leg, sc in the opposite side of next 3 ch [54]
Crochet an additional 12 sc to move the beginning of the round to the side of the body and mark the last stitch you made. This is the new beginning of the round.
Rnd 2 – 7: sc in all 54 st [54]
> *Note: make sure the legs are stuffed firmly at this point as it will be difficult to add stuffing when the body is finished.*

Rnd 8: sc in next 8 st, (dec, sc in next 16 st) repeat 2 times, dec, sc in next 8 st [51]
Rnd 9: (sc in next 15 st, dec) repeat 3 times [48]
Rnd 10: sc in next 7 st, (dec, sc in next 14 st) repeat 2 times, dec, sc in next 7 st [45]
Rnd 11: (sc in next 13 st, dec) repeat 3 times [42]
Change to turquoise yarn.
Rnd 12: sc in all 42 st [42]
Rnd 13: BLO sc in all 42 st [42]
Rnd 14: sc in all 42 st [42]
Change to grass green yarn.
Rnd 15: sc in all 42 st [42]
Rnd 16: sc in next 6 st, (dec, sc in next 12 st) repeat 2 times, dec, sc in next 6 st [39]
Rnd 17: (sc in next 11 st, dec) repeat 3 times [36]
Rnd 18: sc in next 5 st, (dec, sc in next 10 st) repeat 2 times, dec, sc in next 5 st [33]
Rnd 19: (sc in next 9 st, dec) repeat 3 times [30]
Rnd 20: sc in all 30 st [30]
Fasten off, leaving a long tail for sewing. Stuff the body very firmly with fiberfill.

BOTTOM PART OF THE BLOUSE
❋ *start in turquoise yarn*

Ch 42 and join with a slst to make a circle. Make sure the chain isn't twisted.
Rnd 1: sc in all 42 ch [42]
Rnd 2: sc in next 3 st, (inc in next st, sc in next 6 st) repeat 5 times, inc in next st, sc in next 3 st [48]
> *Note: Try it on, the circle should fit the body nicely on the turquoise part. If it's too tight, consider using a bigger hook. If it's too loose, you might want to use a smaller hook.*

Change to grass green yarn.
Rnd 3: (sc in next 15 st, inc in next st) repeat 3 times [51]

Rnd 4: sc in next 8 st, (inc in next st, sc in next 16 st) repeat 2 times, inc in next st, sc in next 8 st [54]

Rnd 5: (sc in next 17 st, inc in next st) repeat 3 times [57]

Rnd 6: sc in next 9 st, (inc in next st, sc in next 18 st) repeat 2 times, inc in next st, sc in next 9 st [60]

Rnd 7: (sc in next 19 st, inc in next st) repeat 3 times [63]

Rnd 8 – 9: sc in all 63 st [63]

Rnd 10: sc in next 10 st, (inc in next st, sc in next 20 st) repeat 2 times, inc in next st, sc in next 10 st [66]

Rnd 11 – 12: sc in all 66 st [66]

Rnd 13: slst in all 66 st [66]

Fasten off and weave in the yarn end. Position the bottom part of the blouse to the leftover front loops of round 12 of the body and sew it on.

HEAD
* in light brown yarn

> **Note:** Unlike most of the heads in this book, Maja's head is crocheted from the bottom to the top because it's ¾ covered with hair, so we think it's a good idea to hide the decreases

underneath (decreases are usually more noticeable than increases).

Rnd 1: start 6 sc in a magic ring [6]

Rnd 2: inc in all 6 st [12]

Rnd 3: (sc in next st, inc in next st) repeat 6 times [18]

Rnd 4: sc in next st, (inc in next st, sc in next 2 st) repeat 5 times, inc in next st, sc in next st [24]

Rnd 5: (sc in next 3 st, inc in next st) repeat 6 times [30]

Rnd 6: work this round in BLO, sc in next 2 st, (inc in next st, sc in next 4 st) repeat 5 times, inc in next st, sc in next 2 st [36]

Rnd 7: (sc in next 5 st, inc in next st) repeat 6 times [42]

Rnd 8: sc in next 3 st, (inc in next st, sc in next 6 st) repeat 5 times, inc in next st, sc in next 3 st [48]

Rnd 9 – 24: sc in all 48 st [48]

Rnd 25: sc in next 3 st, (dec, sc in next 6 st) repeat 5 times, dec, sc in next 3 st [42]

Rnd 26: (sc in next 5 st, dec) repeat 6 times [36]

Rnd 27: sc in next 2 st, (dec, sc in next 4 st) repeat 5 times, dec, sc in next 2 st [30]

Stuff the head with fiberfill and continue stuffing as you go.

Rnd 28: (sc in next 3 st, dec) repeat 6 times [24]

Rnd 29: sc in next st, (dec, sc in next 2 st) repeat 5 times, dec, sc in next st [18]
Finish stuffing the head very firmly.
Rnd 30: (dec, sc in next st) repeat 6 times [12]
Rnd 31: dec 6 times [6]
Fasten off, leaving a yarn tail. Using a yarn needle, weave the yarn tail through the front loop of each remaining stitch and pull it tight to close. Leave a yarn tail, you'll need it later. Sew the head and the body together using the leftover front loops of round 5 of the head. Stuff the neck area with more fiberfill before closing the seam (using a chopstick).

ARM

* make 2, in light brown yarn

Rnd 1: start 6 sc in a magic ring [6]
Rnd 2: (inc in next st, sc in next st) repeat 3 times [9]
Rnd 3: sc in all 9 st [9]
Rnd 4: sc in next 4 st, 4-dc-bobble in next st, sc in next 4 st [9]
Rnd 5 – 19: sc in all 9 st [9]
Stuff only the lower half of the arm with fiberfill, so the arms don't stick out too much after sewing. Make a couple of additional sc or undo a few to get to the opposite side of the thumb. Flatten the arm and work the next round through both layers to close.
Rnd 20: sc in next 4 st [4]
Fasten off, leaving a long tail for sewing. Sew the arms to round 18 of the body.

HAIR

Maja is famous for her heart-shaped hairdo. Crocheting Maja's hair will take quite a bit of work. First, you need to create the base for the hair which will then be covered with curls.
The base of the hair consists of three parts: two round shapes at the top and a flat part at the back.

BASE SHAPE OF THE HAIR

* make 2, in graphite yarn

Rnd 1: start 8 sc in a magic ring [8]
Rnd 2: BLO hdc inc in all 8 st [16]
Rnd 3: BLO (hdc inc in next st, hdc in next st) repeat 8 times [24]
Rnd 4: work this round in BLO, hdc in next 23 st, sc in next st [24]
Fasten off on the first part, leaving a yarn tail. You'll need it to secure the hair to the head later. Don't fasten off on the second part. In the next round, we'll join both parts together (picture 1).
Rnd 5: work this round in BLO, join to the first part with a sc, hdc in the next 23 st on the first part, sc in the first st of the second part, hdc in next 23 st on the second part [48]
Rnd 6 – 10: BLO hdc in all 48 st [48] (picture 2)
Flatten your work and mark the 19 stitches in the middle, this section will form the forehead and will be left unworked (picture 3). Make a few more BLO hdc to reach the closest stitch marker. Ch 1, turn. Continue crocheting the back part of the hair in rows.
Row 1: FLO hdc in all 29 st, ch 1, turn [29]
Row 2: BLO hdc in all 29 st, ch 1, turn [29]
Row 3 – 6: repeat rows 1 and 2 alternately [29]
Don't fasten off. Continue making the curls.
> **Note:** The base of the hair should look like a funny medieval bonnet (pictures 4-5).

CURLS

- To make the curls, you work (ch 7, slst in next st) in all remaining front loops of rows 6-1 of the back part and all around the top of the hair (pictures 6-8).
- Next, bring the graphite yarn tail you left at the end of round 4 of the base of the hair to the front. Position the hair onto the head. Using your hook, pull the light brown yarn tail left from finishing the head through a space between the round shapes, and tie a double knot on top of the head using both tails. This secures the hair in this position and helps to create the heart shape (picture 9). Weave in the yarn ends

EAR
⁎ *make 2, in light brown yarn*

Leave a long starting yarn tail.
Rnd 1: start 5 sc in a magic ring [5]
Pull the magic ring tightly closed and fasten off, leaving a tail for sewing. Sew the ears to both sides of the head, right under the edge of the fringe. Weave in the yarn ends.

COLLAR
⁎ *in off-white yarn*

Ch 19. Crochet in rows.
Row 1: start in second ch from hook, slst in next 18 ch, ch 49, start in second ch from hook, slst in next 18 ch, sc in next 30 ch, ch 2, turn [30]
Continue working on the 30 sc only.
Row 2: 3 hdc in all 30 st, ch 1, turn [90] Leave the remaining stitches unworked.
Row 3: sc in all 90 st [90]
Fasten off and weave in the yarn end.

BOW
⁎ *in lilac yarn*

Diagram 9 on page 135

Leave a long starting yarn tail.
Rnd 1: start (ch 4, 4 tr, ch 4, slst) repeat 2 times in a magic ring.
Pull the magic ring tightly closed. Fasten off, leaving a long tail for sewing. Wrap the yarn tails around the center of your work to create the bow shape and tie a knot with the tails to secure it.

CAT SHOULDER BAG
⁎ *in mauve yarn*

Rnd 1: start 6 sc in a magic ring [6]
Rnd 2: inc in all 6 st [12]
Rnd 3: (sc in next st, inc in next st) repeat 6 times [18]
Rnd 4 – 6: sc in all 18 st [18]

• Pin the hair to the head. The lower edge of the back part should be at round 10 and the fringe should be at round 24 (picture 10). Stuff the round shapes of the hair with fiberfill (make sure they're both stuffed identically, so it looks like a heart, not a mountain range). Also stuff the back part of the hair a little bit (picture 11). When you're happy with the shape, sew all around the hair using single strands of graphite yarn.

9

10

11

Rnd 7: (dec, sc in next st) repeat 6 times [12]
Stuff the bag firmly with fiberfill.
Rnd 8: dec 6 times [6]
Fasten off, leaving a yarn tail. Using a yarn needle, weave the yarn tail through the front loop of each remaining stitch and pull it tight to close. Weave in the yarn end.

STRAP
✳ *in mauve yarn*

Ch 61. Crochet in rows.
Row 1: start in second ch from hook, slst in next 60 ch [60]
Fasten off, leaving a long tail for sewing. Sew the strap to round 7 of the bag.

EAR
✳ *make 2, in mauve yarn*

Leave a long starting yarn tail.
Rnd 1: start sc + hdc + dc + hdc + sc in a magic ring [5]
Pull the magic ring tightly closed. Fasten off, leaving a yarn tail. Sew the ears between rounds 5-7 of the bag. Embroider the cat's snout and eyes on the bag using single strands of graphite yarn. Embroider the cheeks using fuchsia embroidery thread.

FINISHING TOUCHES

• Embroider the facial features. A water-soluble marker or sewing pins may come in handy to mark out the position of the eyes, mouth and cheeks first. The eyes are embroidered using one or two strands of graphite yarn or black embroidery thread. Position the eyes one round below the fringe, with an interspace of approximately 10-11 stitches. Embroider the cheeks underneath the eyes using fuchsia embroidery thread.
• Put the collar around Maja's neck and tie the straps at the back.
• Using the yarn tails, sew the bow to the hair. Weave in the yarn end.
• Put the bag over Maja's shoulder.

HADI

Hadi works as an opera orchestra conductor, where he's referred to as Maestro. He's Gary's partner and Maja's dad. He loves music so much, he even hosts music evenings in his spare time, inviting every neighbor who can play an instrument to join in.

SKILL LEVEL

* * *

SIZE

10.5" / 27.5 cm tall when made with the indicated yarn.

MATERIALS

- Fingering weight yarn in
  • light brown
  • graphite
  • gray
  • turquoise
  • brick brown
  • off-white
  • black (leftover)
- Scraps of black and fuchsia yarn or embroidery thread for the embroidery
- 7 steel / 1.5 mm crochet hook
- Sewing needle
- Yarn needle
- Pins
- 2 flat buttons (diameter 0.5" / 1.4 cm) to strengthen the feet
- Stitch markers
- Fiberfill for stuffing

Scan or visit
www.amigurumi.com/3910
to share pictures and find inspiration.

LEG

✳ *make 2, start in black yarn*

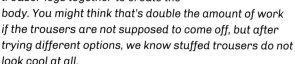

> **Note:** *Hadi has fake trousers that are similar to Oma's trousers. We start by crocheting the legs and trouser legs separately. We continue by attaching the trouser legs directly to the legs, then join the trouser legs together to create the body. You might think that's double the amount of work if the trousers are not supposed to come off, but after trying different options, we know stuffed trousers do not look cool at all.*

Rnd 1: start 6 sc in a magic ring [6]
Rnd 2: inc in all 6 st [12]
Rnd 3: (sc in next st, inc in next st) repeat 6 times [18]
Rnd 4: BLO sc in all 18 st [18]
Rnd 5: sc in all 18 st [18]

> **Note:** *Insert a flat button inside the foot at this point. It's important to keep the soles flat as we want them to have the same shape as cute little hooves.*

Rnd 6: (dec, sc in next st) repeat 6 times [12]
Change to light brown yarn. Stuff the leg very firmly with fiberfill and continue stuffing as you go.

> **Note:** *As the trousers are long and are not coming off, you won't be able to see much of the legs, so it would be smart and eco-friendly to use leftover yarn or yarn in an unpopular color from round 10 up.*

Rnd 7 – 40: sc in all 12 st [12]
Rnd 41: (sc in next 3 st, inc in next st) repeat 3 times [15]
Rnd 42: sc in next 2 st, (inc in next st, sc in next 4 st) repeat 2 times, inc in next st, sc in next 2 st [18]
Rnd 43: (sc in next 5 st, inc in next st) repeat 3 times [21]
Rnd 44: sc in next 3 st, (inc in next st, sc in next 6 st) repeat 2 times, inc in next st, sc in next 3 st [24]
Rnd 45: (sc in next 7 st, inc in next st) repeat 3 times [27]
Fasten off and weave in the yarn end. Make sure the leg is stuffed very firmly and evenly. Set the legs aside and make the trouser legs.

TROUSER LEG

⁕ make 2, in gray yarn

Leave a very long starting yarn tail. You're going to need it to work another round around the bottom of the trouser leg later.

Ch 27 and join with a slst to make a circle. Make sure the chain isn't twisted.

Rnd 1: sc in all 27 ch [27]

Rnd 2 – 40: sc in all 27 st [27]

Don't fasten off. Go back to round 1 and, using the yarn tail you left at the beginning, work slst around the bottom of the trouser leg. Fasten off and weave in the yarn end on the wrong side of your work.

Continue working on round 40. Position the trouser leg over the leg and align the edges. In the next round, we'll join the leg and the trouser leg together.

Rnd 41: sc in all 27 st through both layers [27]

Fasten off, leaving a yarn tail. Join the second leg and trouser leg in the same way, but don't fasten off. In the next round, we'll join both trouser legs together and start crocheting the body.

BODY

⁕ continue in gray yarn

Rnd 1: join to the first trouser leg with a sc, sc in next 26 st on the first trouser leg, sc in next 27 st on the second trouser leg [54] (picture 1)

Crochet an additional 14 sc to move the beginning of the round to the side of the body and mark the last stitch you made. This is the new beginning of the round.

Rnd 2 – 3: sc in all 54 st [54]

Change to turquoise yarn.

Rnd 4: sc in all 54 st [54]

Rnd 5: work this round in BLO, sc in next 4 st, (inc in next st, sc in next 8 st) repeat 5 times, inc in next st, sc in next 4 st [60]

Rnd 6: (sc in next 9 st, inc in next st) repeat 6 times [66]

Rnd 7 – 8: sc in all 66 st [66]

Continue crocheting in a tapestry pattern, alternating

turquoise and graphite yarn. Make sure that the patterned section (29 stitches wide) is centered, and make a couple of additional stitches or undo a few if needed. The color change is indicated in italics before each part and you can refer to the chart below as well.

Rnd 9: {turquoise} sc in next 2 st, ({graphite} sc in next st, {turquoise} sc in next 5 st) repeat 4 times, {graphite} sc in next st, {turquoise} sc in next 39 st [66]

Rnd 10: {turquoise} sc in next st, ({graphite} sc in next 3 st, {turquoise} sc in next 3 st) repeat 4 times, {graphite} sc in next 3 st, {turquoise} sc in next 38 st [66]

Rnd 11: ({graphite} sc in next 5 st, {turquoise} sc in next st) repeat 4 times, {graphite} sc in next 5 st, {turquoise} sc in next 37 st [66]

Rnd 12: {graphite} sc in next 2 st, ({turquoise} sc in next st, {graphite} sc in next 5 st) repeat 4 times, {turquoise} sc in next st, {graphite} sc in next 2 st, {turquoise} sc in next 37 st [66] (pictures 2-4)

Take a break to make the sweater vest ribbing (you can save it for last, but we find it easier to do while the doll is unstuffed). Hold the body with the legs pointing away from you and pull up a loop of brick brown yarn in the last unworked front loop of round 4 of the body. Ch 2, dc in all 54 unworked front loops of round 4, slst in first st. Fasten off and weave in the yarn end. Continue crocheting the body in a tapestry pattern, alternating graphite, brick brown and turquoise yarn.

Rnd 13: ({graphite} sc in next 5 st, {brick brown} sc in next st) repeat 4 times, {graphite} sc in next 5 st, {turquoise} sc in next 37 st [66]

Rnd 14: {brick brown} sc in next st, ({graphite} sc in next 3 st, {brick brown} sc in next 3 st) repeat 4 times, {graphite} sc in next 3 st, {brick brown} sc in next st, {turquoise} sc in next 37 st [66]

Rnd 15: {brick brown} sc in next 2 st, ({graphite} sc in next st, {brick brown} sc in next 5 st) repeat 4 times, {graphite} sc in next st, {brick brown} sc in next 2 st, {turquoise} sc in next 37 st [66]

Rnd 16: ({brick brown} sc in next 5 st, {graphite} sc in next st) repeat 4 times, {brick brown} sc in next 5 st, {turquoise} sc in next 37 st [66]

Rnd 17: {brick brown} sc in next 2 st, ({graphite} sc in next st, {brick brown} sc in next 5 st) repeat 4 times, {graphite} sc in next st, {brick brown} sc in next 2 st, {turquoise} sc in next 37 st [66]

Rnd 18: {brick brown} sc in next st, ({graphite} sc in next 3 st, {brick brown} sc in next 3 st) repeat 4 times, {graphite} sc in next 3 st, {brick brown} sc in next st, {turquoise} sc in next 37 st [66]

Rnd 19: ({graphite} sc in next 5 st, {brick brown} sc in next st) repeat 4 times, {graphite} sc in next 5 st, {turquoise} sc in next 37 st [66]

Fasten off the brick brown yarn.

Rnd 20: {graphite} sc in next 2 st, ({turquoise} sc in next st, {graphite} sc in next 5 st) repeat 4 times, {turquoise} sc in next st, {graphite} sc in next 2 st, {turquoise} sc in next 37 st [66]

Rnd 21: ({graphite} sc in next 5 st, {turquoise} sc in next

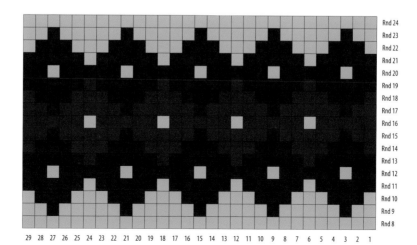

29 28 27 26 25 24 23 22 21 20 19 18 17 16 15 14 13 12 11 10 9 8 7 6 5 4 3 2 1

Rnd 24
Rnd 23
Rnd 22
Rnd 21
Rnd 20
Rnd 19
Rnd 18
Rnd 17
Rnd 16
Rnd 15
Rnd 14
Rnd 13
Rnd 12
Rnd 11
Rnd 10
Rnd 9
Rnd 8

2 times, dec, sc in next 9 st [57]
Rnd 28: (sc in next 17 st, dec) repeat 3 times [54]
Rnd 29: sc in next 8 st, (dec, sc in next 16 st) repeat
2 times, dec, sc in next 8 st [51]
Rnd 30: (sc in next 15 st, dec) repeat 3 times [48]
Rnd 31: sc in next 7 st, (dec, sc in next 14 st) repeat
2 times, dec, sc in next 7 st [45]
Rnd 32: (sc in next 13 st, dec) repeat 3 times [42]
Rnd 33: sc in next 6 st, (dec, sc in next 12 st) repeat
2 times, dec, sc in next 6 st [39]
Rnd 34: (sc in next 11 st, dec) repeat 3 times [36]
Rnd 35: sc in next 5 st, (dec, sc in next 10 st) repeat
2 times, dec, sc in next 5 st [33]
Rnd 36: (sc in next 9 st, dec) repeat 3 times [30]
Fasten off, leaving a long tail for sewing. Stuff the body
very firmly with fiberfill.

HEAD
* *in light brown yarn*

> **Note:** *Unlike most of the heads in this book, Hadi's
> head is crocheted from the bottom to the top be-
> cause it's ¾ covered with hair, so we think it's a good
> idea to hide the decreases underneath (decreases
> are usually more noticeable than increases).*

Rnd 1: start 6 sc in a magic ring [6]
Rnd 2: inc in all 6 st [12]
Rnd 3: (sc in next st, inc in next st) repeat 6 times [18]
Rnd 4: sc in next st, (inc in next st, sc in next 2 st) repeat
5 times, inc in next st, sc in next st [24]
Rnd 5: (sc in next 3 st, inc in next st) repeat 6 times [30]
Rnd 6: BLO (sc in next 9 st, inc in next st) repeat
3 times [33]
Rnd 7: sc in next 5 st, (inc in next st, sc in next 10 st)
repeat 2 times, inc in next st, sc in next 5 st [36]
Rnd 8: (sc in next 11 st, inc in next st) repeat 3 times [39]
Rnd 9: sc in next 6 st, (inc in next st, sc in next 12 st)
repeat 2 times, inc in next st, sc in next 6 st [42]
Rnd 10: (sc in next 13 st, inc in next st) repeat 3 times [45]
Rnd 11: sc in next 7 st, (inc in next st, sc in next 14 st)
repeat 2 times, inc in next st, sc in next 7 st [48]
Rnd 12 – 28: sc in all 48 st [48]
Rnd 29: sc in next 3 st, (dec, sc in next 6 st) repeat
5 times, dec, sc in next 3 st [42]

st) repeat 4 times, *{graphite}* sc in next 5 st, *{turquoise}*
sc in next 37 st [66]
Rnd 22: *{turquoise}* sc in next st, (*{graphite}* sc in next 3 st,
{turquoise} sc in next 3 st) repeat 4 times, *{graphite}*
sc in next 3 st, *{turquoise}* sc in next 38 st [66]
Rnd 23: *{turquoise}* sc in next 2 st, (*{graphite}* sc in next
st, *{turquoise}* sc in next 5 st) repeat 4 times, *{graphite}*
sc in next st, *{turquoise}* sc in next 39 st [66]
Fasten off the graphite yarn, continue working with
turquoise yarn.
Rnd 24: sc in all 66 st [66]
Rnd 25: sc in next 10 st, (dec, sc in next 20 st) repeat
2 times, dec, sc in next 10 st [63]
Rnd 26: (sc in next 19 st, dec) repeat 3 times [60]
Rnd 27: sc in next 9 st, (dec, sc in next 18 st) repeat

Stuff the head firmly with fiberfill and continue stuffing as you go.

Rnd 30: (sc in next 5 st, dec) repeat 6 times [36]

Rnd 31: sc in next 2 st, (dec, sc in next 4 st) repeat 5 times, dec, sc in next 2 st [30]

Rnd 32: (sc in next 3 st, dec) repeat 6 times [24]

Rnd 33: sc in next st, (dec, sc in next 2 st) repeat 5 times, dec, sc in next st [18]

Finish stuffing the head very firmly.

Rnd 34: (dec, sc in next st) repeat 6 times [12]

Rnd 35: dec 6 times [6]

Fasten off, leaving a yarn tail. Using a yarn needle, weave the yarn tail through the front loop of each remaining stitch and pull it tight to close. Leave a yarn tail, you'll need it later. Sew the body to the leftover front loops of round 5 of the head. Stuff the neck area with more fiberfill before closing the seam (using a chopstick).

ARM

∗ *make 2, start in light brown yarn*

Rnd 1: start 5 sc in a magic ring [5]

Rnd 2: inc in all 5 st [10]

Rnd 3: sc in all 10 st [10]

Rnd 4: sc in next 4 st, 5-dc-bobble in next st, sc in next 5 st [10]

Rnd 5 – 9: sc in all 10 st [10]

Change to off-white yarn.

> **Note:** Make sure the color change is at the inside of the arm, add a few sc or undo a few to get to this point.

Rnd 10: BLO sc in all 10 st [10]

Rnd 11: spike st in all 10 st [10]

Rnd 12: BLO sc in all 10 st [10]

Rnd 13 – 37: sc in all 10 st [10]

Stuff only the lower half of the arm with fiberfill, so the arms don't stick out too much after sewing. Make a couple of additional sc or undo a few to get to the opposite side of the thumb. Flatten the arm and work the next round through both layers to close

Rnd 38: sc in all 5 st [5]

Fasten off, leaving a long tail for sewing. Sew the arms to the sides of the body, at 4-5 rounds below the neckline.

HAIR

Hadi's hair is similar to Maja's, but it's smaller and has a simpler shape. First, you create the base for the hair which will then be covered with curls.

The base of the hair consists of two parts: a round shape at the top and a rectangular part at the back.

BASE SHAPE OF THE HAIR

∗ *in graphite yarn*

Rnd 1: start 6 sc in a magic ring [6]

Rnd 2: inc in all 6 st [12]

Rnd 3: BLO hdc inc in all 12 st [24]

Rnd 4: BLO (hdc in next st, hdc inc in next st) repeat 12 times [36]

Rnd 5: BLO (hdc in next 2 st, hdc inc in next st) repeat 12 times [48]

Rnd 6: BLO hdc in all 48 st [48]

Rnd 7: BLO hdc in all 48 st, ch 1, turn [48]

Continue crocheting the back part of the hair in rows.

Row 1: FLO hdc in next 27 st, ch 1, turn [27] Leave the remaining stitches unworked, these form the fringe.

Row 2: BLO hdc in next 27 st, ch 1, turn [27]

Row 3 – 7: repeat rows 1 and 2 alternately [27]

Don't fasten off yet.

> **Note:** Try the hair on the head. It can be a little bit tight, but it should expand a bit when adding the curls. You can add a row or 2 in case you're worried the hair will come out too short.

CURLS

To make the curls, turn the base and, working on the right side with the open side downwards, crochet (ch 4, slst in next st) in all unworked loops of rows 7 to 1. When you reach the top part, crochet (ch 6, slst in next st) in all unworked loops of rounds 7 to 2 (pictures 5-6). Fasten off, leaving a yarn tail.

Position the hair to the head and, using your hook, pull the light brown yarn tail left from finishing the head

through the magic ring of the hair piece. Tie a double knot on top of the head using both tails. This secures the hair in the proper position. Weave in the yarn ends. Pin the hair to the head. The hair doesn't need additional stuffing. When you're happy with the position, sew all around the hair using single strands of graphite yarn.

EAR
* *make 2, in light brown yarn*

Leave a long starting yarn tail.
Rnd 1: start 7 sc in a magic ring [7]
Pull the magic ring tightly closed and fasten off, leaving a tail for sewing. Sew the ears to both sides of the head, between the curls, at 3-5 rounds below the edge of the fringe. Weave in the yarn ends (picture 7).

COLLAR
* *in off-white yarn*

Diagram 5 on page 135

Ch 34. Crochet in rows.
Row 1: start in second ch from hook, sc in next 13 ch, ch 4, start in second ch from hook, sc in next 3 ch, sc in next 7 ch, ch 4, start in second ch from hook, sc in next 3 ch, sc in next 13 ch, ch 1, turn [47]
Row 2: slst in next 10 st, skip next 2 st, dc in next 3 st, 6 dc in next st, dc in next 3 st, skip next 2 st, slst in next st, skip next 2 st, dc in next 3 st, 6 dc in next st, dc in next 3 st, skip next 2 st, slst in next 10 st [45]
Fasten off, leaving a long tail for sewing.

BOW TIE
* *in black yarn*

Diagram 9 on page 135

Leave a long starting yarn tail.
Rnd 1: start (ch 4, 4 tr, ch 4, slst) repeat 2 times in a magic ring.
Pull the magic ring tightly closed. Fasten off, leaving a long tail for sewing. Wrap the yarn tails around the center of your work to create the bow shape and tie a knot with the tails to secure it, leaving a yarn tail for sewing.

FINISHING TOUCHES

- Wrap the collar around Hadi's neck and sew it to the back of the body.
- Using the yarn tails, secure the bow on the body, in the center of the collar opening.
- Embroider the facial features. A water-soluble marker or sewing pins may come in handy to mark out the position of the eyes, eyebrows, mouth and cheeks first. The eyes are embroidered using one or two strands of graphite yarn or black embroidery thread. Position the eyes 5 rounds below the fringe, with an interspace of approximately 12-13 stitches. Embroider the mouth between the eyes, 1-2 rounds below them. Embroider the cheeks underneath the eyes using fuchsia embroidery thread.
- Using a double strand of split turquoise yarn, embroider long stitches to join the light dots of the tapestry pattern on the sweater vest to make it more authentic and lively (picture 8).

MARTHA

Creative and adventurous, Martha is the courageous one amongst her friends! She always comes up with trips into the woods where no other child would dare to go. She also has her own mini curiosity cabinet in the backyard where she stores all her wild findings, like special rocks and shiny bugs.

SKILL LEVEL

*

SIZE

6.5" / 16.5 cm tall when made with the indicated yarn.

MATERIALS

- Fingering weight yarn in:
  • powder pink
  • berry red
  • graphite
  • lavender
  • orange
  • off-white (leftover)
- 7 steel and 4 steel / 1.5 mm and 1.75 mm crochet hook
- Scraps of black, light brown and pink yarn or embroidery thread for the embroidery
- Sewing needle
- Yarn needle
- Pins
- 2 flat buttons (diameter 0.5" / 1,4 cm) to strengthen the feet
- Approx. 8" / 20 cm of blue crafting wire to make the glasses
- 1 small button with 4 holes to attach the wings
- A few tiny buttons in different colors to decorate Martha's T-shirt (may be replaced by beads or French knots)
- Stitch markers
- Fiberfill for stuffing

Scan or visit
www.amigurumi.com/3911
to share pictures and find inspiration.

Note: All parts are worked with a 7 steel / 1.5 mm crochet hook, except for the hair (this is worked with a 4 steel / 1.75 mm crochet hook).

BODY

⁎ *start in berry red yarn*

Rnd 1: start 6 sc in a magic ring [6]
Rnd 2: inc in all 6 st [12]
Rnd 3: (sc in next st, inc in next st) repeat 6 times [18]
Rnd 4: sc in next st, (inc in next st, sc in next 2 st) repeat 5 times, inc in next st, sc in next st [24]
Rnd 5: (sc in next 3 st, inc in next st) repeat 6 times [30]
Rnd 6: sc in next 2 st, (inc in next st, sc in next 4 st) repeat 5 times, inc in next st, sc in next 2 st [36]
Rnd 7: (sc in next 5 st, inc in next st) repeat 6 times [42]
Rnd 8: sc in next 3 st, (inc in next st, sc in next 6 st) repeat 5 times, inc in next st, sc in next 3 st [48]
Rnd 9: (sc in next 7 st, inc in next st) repeat 6 times [54]
Rnd 10: sc in next 4 st, (inc in next st, sc in next 8 st) repeat 5 times, inc in next st, sc in next 4 st [60]
Continue crocheting in a stripe pattern, alternating 1 round in off-white and 3 rounds in berry red yarn.
Rnd 11 – 12: sc in all 60 st [60]
Rnd 13: (sc in next 9 st, inc in next st) repeat 6 times [66]
Rnd 14 – 19: sc in all 66 st [66]
Continue in berry red yarn.
Rnd 20: sc in all 66 st [66]
Rnd 21: sc in next 5 st, (inc in next st, sc in next 10 st) repeat 5 times, inc in next st, sc in next 5 st [72]
Rnd 22: sc in all 72 st [72]
Change to powder pink yarn, but don't fasten off the berry red yarn just yet. Leave it hanging on the outside of your work.
Rnd 23: BLO sc in all 72 st [72]
Rnd 24 – 26: sc in all 72 st [72]
Change to lavender yarn.
Rnd 27: sc in all 72 st [72]
Don't fasten off. Take a break and return to round 22. Using the berry red yarn on the outside of your work, slst in all leftover front loops of this round to make the waist-band of the trousers. Fasten off and weave in the yarn end. Continue working on round 27.

Rnd 28: BLO sc in all 72 st [72]
Rnd 29: (sc in next 10 st, dec) repeat 6 times [66]
Rnd 30: sc in next 10 st, (dec, sc in next 20 st) repeat 2 times, dec, sc in next 10 st [63]
Rnd 31: (sc in next 19 st, dec) repeat 3 times [60]
Rnd 32: sc in next 9 st, (dec, sc in next 18 st) repeat 2 times, dec, sc in next 9 st [57]
Rnd 33: (sc in next 17 st, dec) repeat 3 times [54]
Rnd 34: sc in next 8 st, (dec, sc in next 16 st) repeat 2 times, dec, sc in next 8 st [51]
Rnd 35: (sc in next 15 st, dec) repeat 3 times [48]
Rnd 36: sc in next 7 st, (dec, sc in next 14 st) repeat 2 times, dec, sc in next 7 st [45]
Rnd 37: (sc in next 13 st, dec) repeat 3 times [42]
Change to powder pink yarn, but don't fasten off the lavender yarn just yet and leave it hanging on the outside of your work.
Rnd 38: BLO sc in all 42 st [42]
Rnd 39: (sc in next 5 st, dec) repeat 6 times [36]
Slst in next st. Fasten off, leaving a long tail for sewing. Return to round 37. Using the lavender yarn on the outside of your work, slst in all leftover front loops of round 37 to make the neckline of the T-shirt. Fasten off and weave in the yarn end.
Pull up a loop of lavender yarn in round 27 and slst in all leftover front loops of this round to make the hem of the T-shirt. Fasten off and weave in the yarn end. Stuff the body very firmly with fiberfill.

HEAD
* in powder pink yarn

Rnd 1: start 6 sc in a magic ring [6]
Rnd 2: inc in all 6 st [12]
Rnd 3: (sc in next st, inc in next st) repeat 6 times [18]
Rnd 4: sc in next st, (inc in next st, sc in next 2 st) repeat 5 times, inc in next st, sc in next st [24]
Rnd 5: (sc in next 3 st, inc in next st) repeat 6 times [30]
Rnd 6: sc in next 2 st, (inc in next st, sc in next 4 st) repeat 5 times, inc in next st, sc in next 2 st [36]
Rnd 7: (sc in next 5 st, inc in next st) repeat 6 times [42]
Rnd 8: (sc in next 13 st, inc in next st) repeat 3 times [45]
Rnd 9: sc in next 7 st, (inc in next st, sc in next 14 st) repeat 2 times, inc in next st, sc in next 7 st [48]

Rnd 10: (sc in next 15 st, inc in next st) repeat 3 times [51]
Rnd 11: sc in next 8 st, (inc in next st, sc in next 16 st) repeat 2 times, inc in next st, sc in next 8 st [54]
Rnd 12: (sc in next 17 st, inc in next st) repeat 3 times [57]
Rnd 13: sc in next 9 st, (inc in next st, sc in next 18 st) repeat 2 times, inc in next st, sc in next 9 st [60]
Rnd 14 – 28: sc in all 60 st [60]
Rnd 29: sc in next 4 st, (dec, sc in next 8 st) repeat 5 times, dec, sc in next 4 st [54]
Rnd 30: (sc in next 7 st, dec) repeat 6 times [48]
Stuff the head with fiberfill and continue stuffing as you go.
Rnd 31: sc in next 3 st, (dec, sc in next 6 st) repeat 5 times, dec, sc in next 3 st [42]
Rnd 32: (sc in next 5 st, dec) repeat 6 times [36]
Rnd 33: work this round in BLO, sc in next 2 st, (dec, sc in next 4 st) repeat 5 times, dec, sc in next 2 st [30]
Rnd 34: (sc in next 3 st, dec) repeat 6 times [24]
Rnd 35: sc in next st, (dec, sc in next 2 st) repeat 5 times, dec, sc in next st [18]
Finish stuffing the head very firmly.
Rnd 36: (dec, sc in next st) repeat 6 times [12]
Rnd 37: dec 6 times [6]
Fasten off, leaving a yarn tail. Using a yarn needle, weave the yarn tail through the front loop of each remaining stitch and pull it tight to close. Weave in the yarn end. Sew the head and the body together using the leftover front loops of round 32 of the head. Stuff the neck area with more fiberfill before closing the seam (using a chopstick).

LEG
* make 2, start in graphite yarn

Rnd 1: start 6 sc in a magic ring [6]
Rnd 2: inc in all 6 st [12]
Rnd 3: (sc in next st, inc in next st) repeat 6 times [18]
Rnd 4: BLO sc in all 18 st [18]
Rnd 5: sc in all 18 st [18]
> **Note:** Insert a flat button inside the foot at this point. It's important to keep the soles flat as we want them to have the same shape as cute little hooves.

Rnd 6: (dec, sc in next st) repeat 6 times [12]
Change to powder pink yarn.
Rnd 7 – 13: sc in all 12 st [12]

Change to berry red yarn.
Rnd 14: sc in all 12 st [12]
Rnd 15: FLO inc in all 12 st [24]
Rnd 16: (sc in next 3 st, inc in next st) repeat 6 times [30]
Slst in next st. Fasten off, leaving a long tail for sewing. Stuff the leg very firmly with fiberfill. Sew the legs to the bottom of the body, between rounds 2 and 10 (picture 1).

ARM
* *make 2, start in powder pink yarn*

Rnd 1: start 6 sc in a magic ring [6]
Rnd 2: (sc in next st, inc in next st) repeat 3 times [9]
Rnd 3: sc in all 9 st [9]
Rnd 4: sc in next 4 st, 5-dc-bobble in next st, sc in next 4 st [9]
Rnd 5 – 16: sc in all 9 st [9]
Change to lavender yarn.
> **Note:** *Make sure the color change is at the inside of the arm, add a few sc or undo a few to get to this point.*

Rnd 17: BLO sc in all 9 st [9]
Rnd 18: spike st in all 9 st [9]
Rnd 19: BLO sc in all 9 st [9]
Stuff only the lower half of the arm with fiberfill, so the arms don't stick out too much after sewing. Make a couple of additional sc or undo a few to get to the opposite side of the thumb. Flatten the arm and work the next round through both layers to close.
Rnd 20: sc in all 4 st [4]
Fasten off, leaving a yarn tail for sewing. Sew the arms to the sides of the body, underneath the neckline of the T-shirt.

HAIR
* *in orange yarn, using a 4 steel / 1.75 mm crochet hook*

Rnd 1: start 6 sc in a magic ring [6]
Rnd 2: inc in all 6 st [12]
Rnd 3: (sc in next st, inc in next st) repeat 6 times [18]
Rnd 4: sc in next st, (inc in next st, sc in next 2 st) repeat 5 times, inc in next st, sc in next st [24]

Rnd 5: (sc in next 3 st, inc in next st) repeat 6 times [30]
Rnd 6: sc in next 2 st, (inc in next st, sc in next 4 st) repeat 5 times, inc in next st, sc in next 2 st [36]
Rnd 7: (sc in next 5 st, inc in next st) repeat 6 times [42]
Rnd 8: (sc in next 13 st, inc in next st) repeat 3 times [45]
Rnd 9: sc in next 7 st, (inc in next st, sc in next 14 st) repeat 2 times, inc in next st, sc in next 7 st [48]
Rnd 10 – 11: sc in all 48 st [48]
Rnd 12: (sc in next st, 5-dc-bobble in next st) repeat 24 times [48]
Rnd 13: sc in all 48 st [48]
Rnd 14: (5-dc-bobble in next st, sc in next st) repeat 23 times, 5-dc-bobble in next st, slst in next st, ch 1, turn [48]
Continue crocheting in rows.
Row 1: sc in next 31 st, ch 1, turn [31] Leave the

remaining stitches unworked, these form the fringe.
Row 2: (5-dc-bobble in next st, sc in next st) repeat
15 times, 5-dc-bobble in next st, ch 1, turn [31]
Row 3: sc in all 31 st, ch 1, turn [31]
Row 4: skip 1 st, (5-dc-bobble in next st, sc in next st) repeat 14 times, 5-dc-bobble in next st, slst in next st [30]
Fasten off and weave in the yarn end (pictures 2-3).
Position the hair on Martha's head and pin it in this
position (picture 4). Split a piece of orange yarn into
strands and, using one or two strands, sew the hair
neatly into place.

EAR

* make 2, in powder pink yarn

Leave a long starting yarn tail.
Rnd 1: start 5 sc in a magic ring [5]
Pull the magic ring tightly closed and fasten off, leaving
a tail for sewing. Sew the ears to both sides of the head,
at approximately 5 rounds below the fringe. Weave in
the yarn ends.

FINISHING TOUCHES

• Decorate Martha's T-shirt with tiny buttons or beads in
  different colors. Alternatively, you can use leftover yarn
  to embroider French knots. They will look cute too!

• Embroider the facial features. A water-soluble marker
  or sewing pins may come in handy to mark out the
  position of the eyes, eyebrows, mouth and cheeks first.
  The eyes are embroidered using one or two strands of
  graphite yarn or black embroidery thread. Position the
  eyes 3-4 rounds below the fringe, with an interspace
  of approximately 12-13 stitches. Embroider the mouth
  1 round below the eyes, centered between the eyes.
  Give Martha some freckles by embroidering a few small
  French knots above the mouth, using a single strand
  of orange yarn. Embroider the cheeks underneath the
  eyes using pink embroidery thread. Embroider the eyebrows with light brown yarn.

• To make the glasses, wrap a piece of crafting wire
  around a round object. Skip a section about the distance between the eyes, then wrap the wire around the

round object again, and cut off the excess wire. There should be approximately 1.2" / 3 cm left on the ends for the earpieces. Bend each side and insert the earpieces into the head at 3-4 stitches from each eye (picture 5).

WING

* make 2, in graphite yarn

Leave a long starting yarn tail.
Rnd 1: start 6 sc in a magic ring [6]
Rnd 2: (sc in next st, inc in next st) repeat 3 times [9]
Rnd 3: sc in next st, (inc in next st, sc in next 2 st) repeat 2 times, inc in next st, sc in next st [12]
Rnd 4: (sc in next 3 st, inc in next st) repeat 3 times [15]
Rnd 5: sc in next 2 st, (inc in next st, sc in next 4 st) repeat 2 times, inc in next st, sc in next 2 st [18]
Rnd 6: (sc in next 5 st, inc in next st) repeat 3 times [21]
Pull the starting yarn tail through the magic ring to the outside of your work, you're going to need it to attach the wings to the body.
Rnd 7: sc in next 3 st, (inc in next st, sc in next 6 st) repeat 2 times, inc in next st, sc in next 3 st [24]
Rnd 8: (sc in next 7 st, inc in next st) repeat 3 times [27]
Rnd 9: sc in next 4 st, (inc in next st, sc in next 8 st) repeat 2 times, inc in next st, sc in next 4 st [30]
Rnd 10: (sc in next 9 st, inc in next st) repeat 3 times [33]
Rnd 11: sc in next 5 st, (inc in next st, sc in next 10 st) repeat 2 times, inc in next st, sc in next 5 st [36]
Rnd 12: (sc in next 11 st, inc in next st) repeat 3 times [39]
Rnd 13: sc in next 6 st, (inc in next st, sc in next 12 st) repeat 2 times, inc in next st, sc in next 6 st [42]
Rnd 14: (sc in next 13 st, inc in next st) repeat 3 times [45]
Rnd 15: sc in next 7 st, (inc in next st, sc in next 14 st) repeat 2 times, inc in next st, sc in next 7 st [48]
Rnd 16: (sc in next 15 st, inc in next st) repeat 3 times [51]
Rnd 17: sc in next 8 st, (inc in next st, sc in next 16 st) repeat 2 times, inc in next st, sc in next 8 st [54]
Rnd 18: (sc in next 17 st, inc in next st) repeat 3 times [57]
Rnd 19: sc in next 9 st, (inc in next st, sc in next 18 st) repeat 2 times, inc in next st, sc in next 9 st [60]
Rnd 20: (sc in next 19 st, inc in next st) repeat 3 times [63]
Rnd 21: sc in next 10 st, (inc in next st, sc in next 20 st) repeat 2 times, inc in next st, sc in next 10 st [66]
Rnd 22: (sc in next 21 st, inc in next st) repeat 3 times [69]

Rnd 23: sc in next 11 st, (inc in next st, sc in next 22 st) repeat 2 times, inc in next st, sc in next 11 st [72]
Rnd 24: (sc in next 23 st, inc in next st) repeat 3 times [75]
Rnd 25: sc in next 12 st, (inc in next st, sc in next 24 st) repeat 2 times, inc in next st, sc in next 12 st [78]
The wing doesn't need to be stuffed. Flatten the wing and work the next round through both layers to close.
Rnd 26: sc in next 6 st, hdc in next 4 st, dc in next 3 st, dc + ch-3-picot + dc in next st, dc in next 3 st, hdc in next 2 st, sc in next st, hdc in next 2 st, dc in next 3 st, dc + ch-3-picot + dc in next st, dc in next 3 st, hdc in next 4 st, sc in next 5 st, slst in next st [43] (picture 6)
Fasten off and weave in the yarn end.

- Sew a small flat button with 4 holes in the center back of Martha's T-shirt. Make sure you only use 2 holes to sew it on, as you're going to need the other 2 holes to attach the wings. Pull the yarn tails of both wings through the remaining button holes and make a small bow knot, so you can remove the wings whenever you like (picture 7).
- Using a yarn needle and two pieces of graphite yarn, make ties on the upper outer sections of the wings. Wrap the ties around Martha's wrists and tie them into bow knots.
- Using a yarn needle and a long tail of off-white yarn, make ties for Martha's pants to make sure they don't come off at the worst possible time. Make stitches just below the waistband. Each stitch should be 2 sc long (picture 8). Make a neat bow knot at the front.

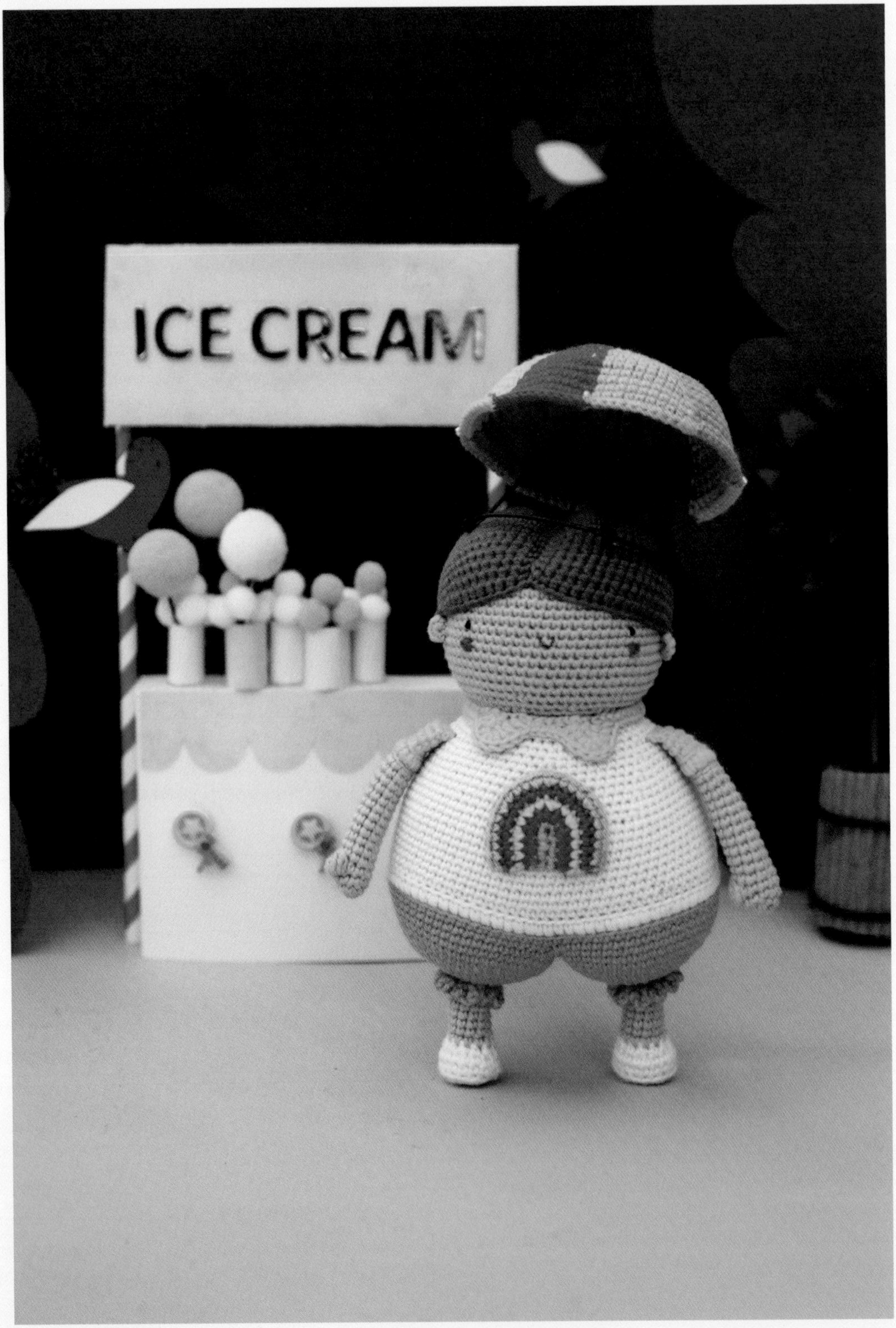
ICE CREAM

TOBI

Tobi is Lula's school friend. He enjoys socializing over good food and has been appointed as the n° 1 party planner. He loves showing off his cooking skills, especially since he went on a summer trip to Italy and learned all about the art of pasta.

SKILL LEVEL

✷ ✷ (✷ headpiece)

SIZE

6.8" / 17.5 cm tall when made with the indicated yarn.

MATERIALS

- Fingering weight yarn in
  • peach
  • off-white
  • mustard yellow
  • azure
  • light brown
  • orange
  • fuchsia
  • lilac (leftover)
  • light green (leftover)
- 7 and 4 steel / 1.5 and 1.75 mm crochet hooks
- Scraps of black and pink yarn or embroidery thread for the embroidery
- Sewing needle
- Yarn needle
- Pins
- 8 tiny beads and 1 small button to decorate the umbrella headpiece
- 2 flat buttons (diameter 0.5" / 1,4 cm) to strengthen the feet
- 23" / 60 cm of crafting wire to make the umbrella headpiece
- 1 flat button with 4 holes to make the umbrella structure
- Hot glue
- Pliers
- Stitch markers
- Fiberfill for stuffing

Scan or visit
www.amigurumi.com/3912
to share pictures and find inspiration.

Note: *All parts are worked with a 7 steel / 1.5 mm crochet hook, except for the umbrella headpiece (this is worked with a 4 steel / 1.75 mm crochet hook).*

HEAD

✳ *in peach yarn*

Rnd 1: start 6 sc in a magic ring [6]
Rnd 2: inc in all 6 st [12]
Rnd 3: (sc in next st, inc in next st) repeat 6 times [18]
Rnd 4: sc in next st, (inc in next st, sc in next 2 st) repeat 5 times, inc in next st, sc in next st [24]
Rnd 5: (sc in next 3 st, inc in next st) repeat 6 times [30]
Rnd 6: sc in next 2 st, (inc in next st, sc in next 4 st) repeat 5 times, inc in next st, sc in next 2 st [36]
Rnd 7: (sc in next 5 st, inc in next st) repeat 6 times [42]
Rnd 8: sc in next 3 st, (inc in next st, sc in next 6 st) repeat 5 times, inc in next st, sc in next 3 st [48]
Rnd 9: (sc in next 7 st, inc in next st) repeat 6 times [54]
Rnd 10: sc in next 4 st, (inc in next st, sc in next 8 st) repeat 5 times, inc in next st, sc in next 4 st [60]
Rnd 11: (sc in next 9 st, inc in next st) repeat 6 times [66]
Rnd 12 – 23: sc in all 66 st [66]
Rnd 24: (sc in next 9 st, dec) repeat 6 times [60]
Rnd 25: sc in next 4 st, (dec, sc in next 8 st) repeat 5 times, dec, sc in next 4 st [54]
Stuff the head with fiberfill and continue stuffing as you go.
Rnd 26: (sc in next 7 st, dec) repeat 6 times [48]
Rnd 27: work this round in BLO, sc in next 3 st, (dec, sc in next 6 st) repeat 5 times, dec, sc in next 3 st [42]
Rnd 28: (sc in next 5 st, dec) repeat 6 times [36]
Rnd 29: sc in next 2 st, (dec, sc in next 4 st) repeat 5 times, dec, sc in next 2 st [30]
Rnd 30: (sc in next 3 st, dec) repeat 6 times [24]
Rnd 31: sc in next st, (dec, sc in next 2 st) repeat 5 times, dec, sc in next st [18]
Finish stuffing the head very firmly.
Rnd 32: (dec, sc in next st) repeat 6 times [12]
Rnd 33: dec 6 times [6]
Fasten off, leaving a yarn tail. Using a yarn needle, weave the yarn tail through the front loop of each remaining stitch and pull it tight to close. Weave in the yarn end.

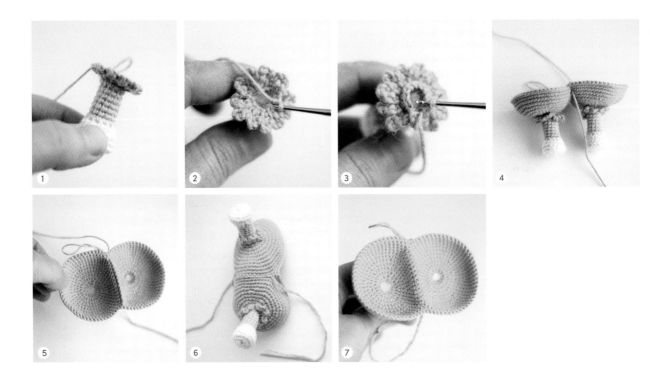

LEG
* make 2, start in off-white yarn

....

Rnd 1: start 6 sc in a magic ring [6]
Rnd 2: inc in all 6 st [12]
Rnd 3: (sc in next st, inc in next st) repeat 6 times [18]
Rnd 4: BLO sc in all 18 st [18]
Rnd 5: sc in all 18 st [18]
> **Note:** *Insert a flat button inside the foot at this point. It's important to keep the soles flat as we want them to have the same shape as cute little hooves.*

Rnd 6: (sc in next st, dec) repeat 6 times [12]
Change to peach yarn.
Rnd 7 – 12: sc in all 12 st [12]
Change to mustard yellow yarn. Stuff the leg firmly with fiberfill and continue stuffing as you go.
Rnd 13: sc in all 12 st [12]
Rnd 14: FLO (ch 4, sc in next st) repeat 12 times [12] (picture 1) This round creates the ruffle of Tobi's pants.
Rnd 15: work this round in the remaining back loops of Rnd 13: sc in all 12 st [12] (pictures 2-3)

Rnd 16: inc in all 12 st [24]
Rnd 17: (sc in next 3 st, inc in next st) repeat 6 times [30]
Rnd 18: sc in next 2 st, (inc in next st, sc in next 4 st) repeat 5 times, inc in next st, sc in next 2 st [36]
Rnd 19: (sc in next 5 st, inc in next st) repeat 6 times [42]
Rnd 20: sc in next 3 st, (inc in next st, sc in next 6 st) repeat 5 times, inc in next st, sc in next 3 st [48]
Rnd 21: (sc in next 7 st, inc in next st) repeat 6 times [54]
Rnd 22 – 24: sc in all 54 st [54]
Fasten off on the first leg, leaving a yarn tail. Don't fasten off on the second leg. Mark the 13th stitch of round 24. In the next round, we'll join both legs together and start crocheting the body (picture 4).

BODY
* continue in mustard yellow yarn

....

Rnd 1: join to the first leg with a sc, sc in next 41 st on the first leg, skip the remaining 12 st, skip 12 st on the second leg, sc in the 13th st of the second leg, sc in next 41 st on the second leg [84]

Rnd 2: sc in all 84 st [84]

Crochet an additional 20 sc to move the beginning of the round to the side of the body and mark the last stitch you made. This will be the new beginning of the round.

> *Note: You don't need military precision here because the doll is pretty big. If you miscalculated and missed a stitch or made an extra one, don't get upset, just make an increase or a decrease in the next round to reach the correct number of stitches.*

Change to off-white yarn. Use the yarn tail left on the first leg to sew the gap between the legs closed (pictures 5-7).

Rnd 3: BLO sc in all 84 st [84]

Rnd 4: spike st in all 84 st [84]

Rnd 5: BLO sc in all 84 st [84]

Rnd 6 – 14: sc in all 84 st [84]

Rnd 15: sc in next 13 st, (dec, sc in next 26 st) repeat 2 times, dec, sc in next 13 st [81]

Rnd 16: (sc in next 25 st, dec) repeat 3 times [78]

Rnd 17: sc in next 12 st, (dec, sc in next 24 st) repeat 2 times, dec, sc in next 12 st [75]

Rnd 18: (sc in next 23 st, dec) repeat 3 times [72]

Rnd 19: sc in next 11 st, (dec, sc in next 22 st) repeat 2 times, dec, sc in next 11 st [69]

Rnd 20: (sc in next 21 st, dec) repeat 3 times [66]

Rnd 21: sc in next 10 st, (dec, sc in next 20 st) repeat 2 times, dec, sc in next 10 st [63]

Rnd 22: (sc in next 19 st, dec) repeat 3 times [60]

Rnd 23: sc in next 9 st, (dec, sc in next 18 st) repeat 2 times, dec, sc in next 9 st [57]

Rnd 24: (sc in next 17 st, dec) repeat 3 times [54]

Rnd 25: sc in next 8 st, (dec, sc in next 16 st) repeat 2 times, dec, sc in next 8 st [51]

Rnd 26: (sc in next 15 st, dec) repeat 3 times [48]

Fasten off, leaving a long tail for sewing. Stuff the body very firmly with fiberfill. Sew the head and the body together using the leftover front loops of round 26 of the head. Stuff the neck area with more fiberfill before closing the seam (using a chopstick).

ARM

* *make 2, start in peach yarn*

Rnd 1: start 5 sc in a magic ring [5]

Rnd 2: inc in all 5 st [10]

Rnd 3: sc in all 10 st [10]

Rnd 4: sc in next 4 st, 5-dc-bobble in next st, sc in next 5 st [10]

Rnd 5 – 16: sc in all 10 st [10]

Stuff only the lower half of the arm with fiberfill, so the arms don't stick out too much after sewing. Change to azure yarn.

> *Note: Make sure the color change is at the inside of the arm, add a few sc or undo a few to get to this point.*

Rnd 17: BLO sc in all 10 st [10]

Rnd 18: spike st in all 10 st [10]

Rnd 19: BLO sc in all 10 st [10]

Rnd 20 – 21: sc in all 10 st [10]

Make a couple of additional sc or undo a few to get to the opposite side of the thumb. Flatten the arm and work the next round through both layers to close.

Rnd 22: sc in all 5 st [5]

Fasten off, leaving a yarn tail for sewing. Sew the arms to the sides of the body, between rounds 22 and 23.

HAIR

* *in light brown yarn*

Rnd 1: start 6 sc in a magic ring [6]

Rnd 2: inc in all 6 st [12]

Rnd 3: (sc in next st, inc in next st) repeat 6 times [18]

Rnd 4: sc in next st, (inc in next st, sc in next 2 st) repeat 5 times, inc in next st, sc in next st [24]

Rnd 5: (sc in next 3 st, inc in next st) repeat 6 times [30]

Rnd 6: sc in next 2 st, (inc in next st, sc in next 4 st) repeat 5 times, inc in next st, sc in next 2 st [36]

Rnd 7: (sc in next 5 st, inc in next st) repeat 6 times [42]

Rnd 8: sc in next 3 st, (inc in next st, sc in next 6 st) repeat 5 times, inc in next st, sc in next 3 st [48]

Rnd 9: (sc in next 7 st, inc in next st) repeat 6 times [54]

Rnd 10: sc in next 4 st, (inc in next st, sc in next 8 st) repeat 5 times, inc in next st, sc in next 4 st [60]

Rnd 11: (sc in next 9 st, inc in next st) repeat 6 times [66]

Rnd 12: sc in next 5 st, (inc in next st, sc in next 10 st) repeat 5 times, inc in next st, sc in next 5 st [72]

Rnd 13 – 15: sc in all 72 st [72]

Rnd 16 – 21: sc in next st, hdc in next 18 st, sc in next 42 st, hdc in next 9 st, sc in next st, slst in next st [72]

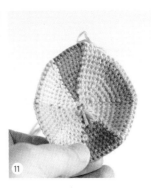

Rnd 22: sc in next 2 st, hdc in next 14 st, sc in next 5 st [21] Leave the remaining stitches unworked.

Fasten off and weave in the yarn end. Position the hair onto the head at an angle of approximately 45°. Secure it with pins. Split the light brown yarn tail into strands and take one or two strands on a yarn needle. Mark the hair parting at the front top of the head with pins. Embroider a few short stitches through hair and head to fix the hair parting (see pictures in Dad's pattern, page 22). Split another yarn piece into strands and use one or two strands to sew the back side of the hair to the head. Add a little bit of fiberfill under the hair to give it some volume (Tobi's hair shouldn't be as voluminous as everyone else's). Make sure the hairdo looks smooth and even and has a nice shape. When you're happy with the way it looks, sew the front part of the hair to the forehead, using one or two strands of light brown yarn.

EAR
* make 2, in peach yarn

Leave a long starting yarn tail.
Rnd 1: start 5 sc in a magic ring [5]
Pull the magic ring tightly closed and fasten off, leaving a tail for sewing. Sew the ears to both sides of the head, right underneath the edge of the hair. Weave in the yarn ends.

COLLAR
* in azure yarn

diagram 6 on page 135

Ch 24. Crochet in rows.
Row 1: start in second ch from hook, sc in next 2 ch, ch 10, start in second ch from hook, sc in next 2 ch, ch 21, ch 1, turn [59]
Row 2: sc in next 19 ch, skip next 2 ch, dc in next 2 st, 5 dc in next ch, dc in next 2 ch, skip next 2 ch, sc in next 3 ch, skip next 2 ch, dc in next 2 st, 5 dc in next ch, dc in next 2 ch, skip next 2 ch, sc in next 19 ch [59]
Fasten off, leaving a long tail for sewing. Wrap the collar around Tobi's neck and sew it to the back with a few stitches.

RAINBOW PRINT
* start in mustard yellow yarn

Ch 5. Crochet in rows.
Row 1: start in second ch from hook, sc in next 3 ch, 4 sc in next ch. Continue on the other side of the foundation chain, sc in next 3 ch, change to fuchsia yarn, ch 1, turn [10]
Row 2: sc in next 3 st, inc in next 4 st, sc in next 3 st, change to azure yarn, ch 1, turn [14]
Row 3: sc in next 3 st, (sc in next st, inc in next st) repeat 4 times, sc in next 3 st, change to lilac yarn, ch 1, turn [18]
Row 4: sc in next 4 st, (inc in next st, sc in next 2 st) re-peat 3 times, inc in next st, sc in next 4 st, change to light green yarn, ch 1, turn [22]
Row 5: sc in next 6 st, inc in next st, sc in next 3 st, inc in

next 2 st, sc in next 3 st, inc in next st, sc in next 6 st [26]
Fasten off and weave in the yarn end (picture 8).

FINISHING TOUCHES

- Embroider the facial features. A water-soluble marker or sewing pins may come in handy to mark out the position of the eyes, mouth and cheeks first. The eyes are embroidered using one or two strands of graphite yarn or black embroidery thread. Positon the eyes on round 17, with an interspace of approximately 16 stitches. Embroider the cheeks underneath the eyes using pink embroidery thread.
- Sew the rainbow print in the center of Tobi's shirt, at 6 rounds from the hem.

UMBRELLA HEADPIECE
✳ *using a 4 steel / 1.75 mm crochet hook*

Note: The umbrella headpiece is worked using alternating colors. The color change is indicated in italics before each part. We recommend using the tapestry crochet technique (tutorial on p. 15) to handle the four yarn colors of this part, to make sure the rainbow piece looks good on both sides. We highly recommend using a bigger hook to make your work easier.

Rnd 1: *{mustard yellow}* start 8 sc in a magic ring [8]
Rnd 2: (*{mustard yellow}* inc in next st, *{azure}* inc in next st, *{fuchsia}* inc in next st, *{orange}* inc in next st) repeat 2 times [16] (picture 9)
Rnd 3: (*{mustard yellow}* sc in next st, inc in next st, *{azure}* sc in next st, inc in next st, *{fuchsia}* sc in next st, inc in next st, *{orange}* sc in next st, inc in next st) repeat 2 times [24]
Rnd 4: (*{mustard yellow}* sc in next 2 st, inc in next st, *{azure}* sc in next 2 st, inc in next st, *{fuchsia}* sc in next 2 st, inc in next st, *{orange}* sc in next 2 st, inc in next st) repeat 2 times [32]
Rnd 5: (*{mustard yellow}* sc in next 3 st, inc in next st, *{azure}* sc in next 3 st, inc in next st, *{fuchsia}* sc in next 3 st, inc in next st, *{orange}* sc in next 3 st, inc in next st) repeat 2 times [40]

Rnd 6: (*{mustard yellow}* sc in next 4 st, inc in next st, *{azure}* sc in next 4 st, inc in next st, *{fuchsia}* sc in next 4 st, inc in next st, *{orange}* sc in next 4 st, inc in next st) repeat 2 times [48]
Rnd 7: (*{mustard yellow}* sc in next 5 st, inc in next st, *{azure}* sc in next 5 st, inc in next st, *{fuchsia}* sc in next 5 st, inc in next st, *{orange}* sc in next 5 st, inc in next st) repeat 2 times [56]
Rnd 8: (*{mustard yellow}* sc in next 7 st, *{azure}* sc in next 7 st, *{fuchsia}* sc in next 7 st, *{orange}* sc in next 7 st) repeat 2 times [56]
Rnd 9: (*{mustard yellow}* sc in next 6 st, inc in next st, *{azure}* sc in next 6 st, inc in next st, *{fuchsia}* sc in next 6 st, inc in next st, *{orange}* sc in next 6 st, inc in next st)

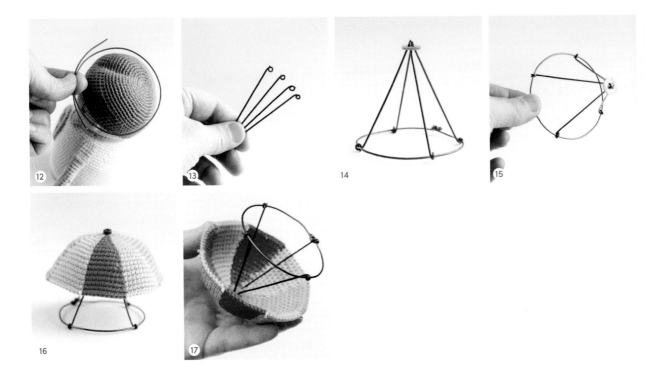

repeat 2 times [64]

Rnd 10: (*{mustard yellow}* sc in next 8 st, *{azure}* sc in next 8 st, *{fuchsia}* sc in next 8 st, *{orange}* sc in next 8 st) repeat 2 times [64]

Rnd 11: (*{mustard yellow}* sc in next 7 st, inc in next st, *{azure}* sc in next 7 st, inc in next st, *{fuchsia}* sc in next 7 st, inc in next st, *{orange}* sc in next 7 st, inc in next st) repeat 2 times [72]

Rnd 12: (*{mustard yellow}* sc in next 9 st, *{azure}* sc in next 9 st, *{fuchsia}* sc in next 9 st, *{orange}* sc in next 9 st) repeat 2 times [72]

Rnd 13: (*{mustard yellow}* sc in next 8 st, inc in next st, *{azure}* sc in next 8 st, inc in next st, *{fuchsia}* sc in next 8 st, inc in next st, *{orange}* sc in next 8 st, inc in next st) repeat 2 times [80]

Rnd 14: (*{mustard yellow}* sc in next 10 st, *{azure}* sc in next 10 st, *{fuchsia}* sc in next 10 st, *{orange}* sc in next 10 st) repeat 2 times [80]

Rnd 15: (*{mustard yellow}* sc in next 9 st, inc in next st, *{azure}* sc in next 9 st, inc in next st, *{fuchsia}* sc in next 9 st, inc in next st, *{orange}* sc in next 9 st, inc in next st) repeat 2 times [88]

Rnd 16: (*{mustard yellow}* sc in next 11 st, *{azure}* sc in next 11 st, *{fuchsia}* sc in next 11 st, *{orange}* sc in next 11 st) repeat 2 times [88]

Fasten off and weave in the yarn end (pictures 10-11). To make the wire structure, make a ring that fits around Tobi's head, but don't close it yet (picture 12). Cut four pieces of wire for the poles with the same length as the diameter of the ring you just made. Using pliers, make a small loop on one side of each pole (picture 13) and slide them on the ring. Arrange the poles nicely and join them at the top using a flat button with four holes and a drop of hot glue (pictures 14-15). Secure the umbrella on the wire structure with another drop of glue. If you think the rainbow part is a little bit too flexible, you can starch and iron it before attaching it to the wire structure. Decorate the umbrella with a small button on top and a tiny bead on each bottom corner (pictures 16-17).

YUHU

Yuhu the Owl lives in Lula's backyard and tries to avoid the kids as much as she can. She's smart and grumpy and is often bothered by the silly little things humans do on a daily basis, like smacking loudly while eating. She does have a soft spot for Bo, since he often gives her earthworms to snack on.

SKILL LEVEL

*

SIZE

4.5" / 11.5 cm tall when made with the indicated yarn.

MATERIALS

- Fingering weight yarn in:
  • baby blue
  • jeans blue
  • burgundy
  • black
  • mustard yellow (leftover)
  • orange (leftover)
  • berry red (leftover)
  • off-white (leftover)
- 7 steel / 1.5 mm crochet hook
- Sewing needle
- Yarn needle
- Pins
- 2 small black beads (diameter 0.6" / 1.5 cm)
- Stitch markers
- Fiberfill for stuffing

Scan or visit
www.amigurumi.com/3913
to share pictures and find inspiration.

HEAD AND BODY
* *start in baby blue yarn*

Rnd 1: start 6 sc in a magic ring [6]
Rnd 2: inc in all 6 st [12]
Rnd 3: (sc in next st, inc in next st) repeat 6 times [18]
Rnd 4: sc in next st, (inc in next st, sc in next 2 st) repeat 5 times, inc in next st, sc in next st [24]
Rnd 5: (sc in next 3 st, inc in next st) repeat 6 times [30]
Rnd 6: sc in next 2 st, (inc in next st, sc in next 4 st) repeat 5 times, inc in next st, sc in next 2 st [36]
Rnd 7: (sc in next 5 st, inc in next st) repeat 6 times [42]
Rnd 8: sc in next 3 st, (inc in next st, sc in next 6 st) repeat 5 times, inc in next st, sc in next 3 st [48]
Rnd 9 – 20: sc in all 48 st [48]
Change to jeans blue yarn.
Rnd 21: sc in all 48 st [48]
Rnd 22: sc in next 31 st, (inc in next st, sc in next 2 st) repeat 5 times, inc in next st, sc in next st [54]
Rnd 23: sc in next 30 st, (sc in next 3 st, inc in next st) repeat 6 times [60]
Rnd 24: sc in next 32 st, (inc in next st, sc in next 4 st) repeat 5 times, inc in next st, sc in next 2 st [66]
Rnd 25 – 36: sc in all 66 st [66] (picture 1)
Rnd 37: (sc in next 9 st, dec) repeat 6 times [60]
Stuff your work with fiberfill and continue stuffing as you go.
Rnd 38: sc in next 4 st, (dec, sc in next 8 st) repeat 5 times, dec, sc in next 4 st [54]
Rnd 39: (sc in next 7 st, dec) repeat 6 times [48]
Rnd 40: sc in next 3 st, (dec, sc in next 6 st) repeat 5 times, dec, sc in next 3 st [42]
Rnd 41: (sc in next 5 st, dec) repeat 6 times [36]
Rnd 42: sc in next 2 st, (dec, sc in next 4 st) repeat 5 times, dec, sc in next 2 st [30]
Rnd 43: (sc in next 3 st, dec) repeat 6 times [24]
Rnd 44: sc in next st, (dec, sc in next 2 st) repeat 5 times, dec, sc in next st [18]
Rnd 45: (dec, sc in next st) repeat 6 times [12]
Finish stuffing the body and head firmly.

> ***Note:*** *make sure that the top of the head and the bottom of the body are nicely shaped in the form of a hemisphere, and that they're not flat or wrinkly.*

Rnd 46: dec 6 times [6]

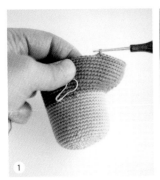

Fasten off, leaving a yarn tail. Using a yarn needle, weave the yarn tail through the front loop of each remaining stitch and pull it tight to close. Weave in the yarn end.

WING
* make 2

SMALL FEATHER
* in burgundy yarn

Rnd 1: start 6 sc in a magic ring [6]
Rnd 2: inc in all 6 st [12]
Rnd 3 – 4: sc in all 12 st [12]
Fasten off and weave in the yarn end. The small feather doesn't need to be stuffed.

LARGE FEATHER
* in burgundy yarn

Rnd 1: start 6 sc in a magic ring [6]
Rnd 2: inc in all 6 st [12]
Rnd 3: (sc in next st, inc in next st) repeat 6 times [18]
Rnd 4: sc in next st, (inc in next st, sc in next 2 st) repeat 5 times, inc in next st, sc in next st [24]
Rnd 5: (sc in next 3 st, inc in next st) repeat 6 times [30]
Rnd 6 – 9: sc in all 30 st [30]
In the next round, we'll join the large and the small feather together.
Rnd 10: sc in next 15 st on the large feather, sc in next 12 st on the small feather, sc in next 15 st on the large

feather [42] (picture 2)
Rnd 11 – 14: sc in all 42 st [42]
Rnd 15: sc in next 6 st, (dec, sc in next 12 st) repeat 2 times, dec, sc in next 6 st [39]
Rnd 16: (sc in next 11 st, dec) repeat 3 times [36]
Rnd 17: sc in next 5 st, (dec, sc in next 10 st) repeat 2 times, dec, sc in next 5 st [33]
Rnd 18: (sc in next 9 st, dec) repeat 3 times [30]
Rnd 19: sc in next 4 st, (dec, sc in next 8 st) repeat 2 times, dec, sc in next 4 st [27]
Rnd 20: (sc in next 7 st, dec) repeat 3 times [24]
Rnd 21: sc in all 24 st [24]
   ***Note:** The finished wing will look like a mitten.*
Don't fasten off yet. Make French knots all over the wings using berry red yarn (picture 3). Don't forget that the wings mirror each other in the end result.
Make a couple of additional sc or undo a few to get to the opposite side of the small feather. The wing doesn't need to be stuffed. Flatten the wing and work the next round through both layers to close.
Rnd 22: sc in all 12 st [12]
Fasten off, leaving a long tail for sewing.

BELLY
* in baby blue yarn

Rnd 1: start 6 sc in a magic ring [6]
Rnd 2: inc in all 6 st [12]
Rnd 3: (sc in next st, inc in next st) repeat 6 times [18]
Rnd 4: sc in next st, (inc in next st, sc in next 2 st) repeat 5 times, inc in next st, sc in next st [24]
Rnd 5: (sc in next 3 st, inc in next st) repeat 6 times [30]

Rnd 6: sc in next 2 st, (inc in next st, sc in next 4 st) repeat 5 times, inc in next st, sc in next 2 st [36]
Rnd 7: (sc in next 5 st, inc in next st) repeat 6 times [42]
Rnd 8: sc in next 3 st, (inc in next st, sc in next 6 st) repeat 5 times, inc in next st, sc in next 3 st [48]
Rnd 9: (sc in next 7 st, inc in next st) repeat 6 times [54]
Rnd 10: sc in next 4 st, (inc in next st, sc in next 8 st) repeat 5 times, inc in next st, sc in next 4 st [60]
Fasten off, leaving a long tail for sewing. Make French knots using baby blue yarn on the right side of the belly.

BEARD
❋ *in black yarn*

> **Note:** *Please note that English is not the first language of yours truly and ornithology is not our specialty either, so we're not even going to try to find the appropriate names of the owl's features. We'll use simple words, such as "beard" and "unibrow" instead, and you can make fun of it :)*

Rnd 1: start 5 sc in a magic ring [5]
Rnd 2: inc in all 5 st [10]
Rnd 3: sc in all 10 st [10]
Rnd 4 – 6: dec, sc in next 2 st, inc in next 2 st, sc in next 2 st, dec [10]
Rnd 7: sc in next 4 st, inc in next 2 st, sc in next 4 st [12]
Rnd 8 – 10: dec, sc in next 3 st, inc in next 2 st, sc in next 3 st, dec [12]
Rnd 11: sc in next 5 st, inc in next 2 st, sc in next 5 st [14]
Rnd 12 – 20: dec, sc in next 4 st, inc in next 2 st, sc in next 4 st, dec [14]
Rnd 21: dec, sc in next 10 st, dec [12]
Rnd 22 – 24: dec, sc in next 3 st, inc in next 2 st, sc in next 3 st, dec [12]
Rnd 25: dec, sc in next 8 st, dec [10]
Rnd 26 – 28: dec, sc in next 2 st, inc in next 2 st, sc in next 2 st, dec [10]
Rnd 29: sc in all 10 st [10]
Stuff the beard lightly with fiberfill.
Rnd 30: dec 5 times [5]
Fasten off, leaving a long tail for sewing. Using a yarn needle, weave the yarn tail through the front loop of each remaining stitch and pull it tight to close. Weave in the yarn end (picture 4).

TAIL
Yuhu's tail consists of three feathers (two small ones on the sides and a big one in the center).

BIG FEATHER
❋ *in black yarn*

Rnd 1: start 6 sc in a magic ring [6]
Rnd 2: inc in all 6 st [12]
Rnd 3 – 5: sc in all 12 st [12]
The big feather doesn't need to be stuffed. Fasten off and weave in the yarn end.

SMALL FEATHER
❋ *make 2, in black yarn*

Rnd 1: start 6 sc in a magic ring [6]
Rnd 2: (sc in next st, inc in next st) repeat 3 times [9]
Rnd 3 – 5: sc in all 9 st [9]
The small feathers don't need to be stuffed. Fasten off on the first feather and weave in the yarn end. Don't fasten off on the second feather.

JOINING THE FEATHERS

In the next round, we'll join the feathers together.
Rnd 1: sc in next 4 st on the second small feather, sc in next 6 st on the big feather, sc in next 9 st on the first small feather, sc in next 6 st on the big feather, sc in next 5 st of the second small feather [30]
Rnd 2: sc in all 30 st [30]
Rnd 3: sc in next 4 st, (dec, sc in next 8 st) repeat 2 times, dec, sc in next 4 st [27]
Rnd 4: (sc in next 7 st, dec) repeat 3 times [24]
Make a couple of additional sc or undo a few to get to the side of the tail. The tail doesn't need to be stuffed. Flatten the tail and work the next round through both layers to close.
Rnd 5: sc in all 12 st [12]
Fasten off, leaving a long tail for sewing.

EAR
* make 2, in black yarn

Rnd 1: start 6 sc in a magic ring [6]
Rnd 2: (sc in next st, inc in next st) repeat 3 times [9]
Rnd 3 – 4: sc in all 9 st [9]
Rnd 5: dec, sc in next 7 st [8]
Rnd 6: sc in next 3 st, dec, sc in next 3 st [7]
Rnd 7: dec, sc in next 5 st [6]
The ears don't need to be stuffed. Fasten off, leaving a long tail. Using a yarn needle, weave the yarn tail through the front loop of each remaining stitch and pull it tight to close. Leave a yarn tail for sewing.

LONG UNIBROW
* in off-white yarn

> **Note:** You can stuff the unibrow lightly as you go (but it's not necessary).

Rnd 1: start 6 sc in a magic ring [6]
Rnd 2: inc in all 6 st [12]
Rnd 3 – 5: sc in all 12 st [12]
Rnd 6: sc in next 5 st, dec, sc in next 5 st [11]
Rnd 7: dec, sc in next 9 st [10]
Rnd 8: sc in next 4 st, dec, sc in next 4 st [9]
Rnd 9 – 18: sc in all 9 st [9]
Rnd 19: sc in next 4 st, inc in next st, sc in next 4 st [10]
Rnd 20: inc in next st, sc in next 9 st [11]
Rnd 21: sc in next 5 st, inc in next st, sc in next 5 st [12]
Rnd 22 – 25: sc in all 12 st [12]
Rnd 26: dec 6 times [6]

Fasten off, leaving a long yarn tail. Using a yarn needle, weave the yarn tail through the front loop of each remaining stitch and pull it tight to close. Weave in the yarn end.

SHORT UNIBROW
* in burgundy yarn

> **Note:** You can stuff the unibrow lightly as you go (but it's not necessary).

Rnd 1: start 6 sc in a magic ring [6]
Rnd 2: (sc in next st, inc in next st) repeat 3 times [9]
Rnd 3 – 4: sc in all 9 st [9]
Rnd 5: dec, sc in next 7 st [8]
Rnd 6: sc in next 3 st, dec, sc in next 3 st [7]
Rnd 7: dec, sc in next 5 st [6]
Rnd 8: sc in all 6 st [6]
Rnd 9: inc in next st, sc in next 5 st [7]
Rnd 10: sc in next 3 st, inc in next st, sc in next 3 st [8]
Rnd 11: inc in next st, sc in next 7 st [9]
Rnd 12 – 14: sc in all 9 st [9]
Rnd 15: (dec, sc in next st) repeat 3 times [6]
Fasten off, leaving a yarn tail. Using a yarn needle, weave the yarn tail through the front loop of each remaining stitch and pull it tight to close. Weave in the yarn end.

EYE
* make 2, in mustard yellow yarn

Crochet in joined rounds.
Rnd 1: start 7 sc in a magic ring, slst in first st, ch 1 [7]

Rnd 2: inc in all 7 st, slst in first st [14]
Fasten off, leaving a yarn tail for sewing.

LEG
* *make 2, in mustard yellow yarn*

Leave a long starting yarn tail.
Rnd 1: ch 10, start in second ch from hook, slst in next 3 ch, (ch 4, start in second ch from hook, slst in next 3 ch) repeat 2 times, slst in next 6 ch [15]
Fasten off, leaving a yarn tail for sewing.

ASSEMBLY AND FINISHING TOUCHES

Note: We've sewn the owl's parts slightly asymmetrically, so the finished character looks more playful and lively and is funnier to photograph.
- Sew the belly patch to the body between rounds 24 and 43 (3-4 rounds below the start of the darker part). Please note that the more prominent part of the body (the one with the increases) is the back.
- Wrap the beard around the head and sew the ends to round 13, with an interspace of 24 stitches at the back (pictures 8-9).
- Sew the wings to the sides of the body (with the top edges on round 21), so the small feathers can touch the belly patch.
- Sew the tail to the back of the body, between rounds 33 and 34.
- Sew small black beads on the eyes to make the pupils.
  Note: We wanted them to be identical, that's why we've used beads, but if Precision is your middle name, you can, of course, make French knots using black yarn instead.
- Pin the facial features to the head and sew them on. The eyes are positioned between rounds 8 and 13 of the head, with an interspace of 6 stitches.
  Note: As the eyes are very small, it's highly recommended to split the yarn tail into strands and use only one of them for sewing.
  The shorter unibrow is positioned between rounds

6 and 8 and the large unibrow is positioned between rounds 8 and 11 (pictures 7-8).
- Sew the ears to the head, right behind the eyes.
- Embroider the beak between the eyes using orange yarn. The beak is 3 stitches wide and 4 stitches long. Embroider cheeks under the eyes using berry red yarn.
- Sew the legs to the body, on top of the belly patch, keeping into account your owl's balance.

STEFAN

Always hardworking and polite, Stefan works for the local post office. You can count on him to deliver each package on time. He likes to leave a caramel mint with every newspaper he delivers, just as a little extra to brighten up your day.

SKILL LEVEL

∗∗

SIZE

9.5" / 24.5 cm tall when made with the indicated yarn.

MATERIALS

- Fingering weight yarn in:
  - graphite
  - mustard yellow
  - nude
  - jeans blue (leftover)
  - light brown (leftover)
- 7 steel / 1.5 mm crochet hook
- Scraps of black and pink yarn or embroidery thread for the embroidery
- Sewing needle
- Yarn needle
- 2 flat buttons (diameter 0.5" / 1,4 cm) to strengthen the feet
- 3 tiny buttons or beads (diameter 1/16" / 2 mm) for the pockets and bag
- 1 small gray button (diameter 1/8" / 4 mm) for the hat
- Stitch markers
- Fiberfill for stuffing

Scan or visit
www.amigurumi.com/3914
to share pictures and find inspiration.

LEG

∗ *make 2, start in jeans blue yarn*

Note: *Stefan has fake trousers that are made in the same way as Oma's trousers. We start by crocheting the legs and trouser legs separately. We continue by attaching the trouser legs directly to the legs, then join the trouser legs together to create the body. You might think that's double the amount of work if the trousers are this long and are not supposed to come off, but we've tried different options and, we swear to the postal gods, stuffed trousers (especially as wide as Stefan's) do not look cool at all.*

Rnd 1: start 7 sc in a magic ring [7]
Rnd 2: inc in all 7 st [14]
Rnd 3: (sc in next st, inc in next st) repeat 7 times [21]
Rnd 4: BLO sc in all 21 st [21]
Rnd 5: sc in all 21 st [21]

Note: *Insert a flat button inside the foot at this point. It's important to keep the soles flat as we want them to have the same shape as cute little hooves.*

Rnd 6: (dec, sc in next st) repeat 7 times [14]

Note: *As the trousers are long and are not coming off, you won't be able to see much of the legs, so it would be smart and eco-friendly to use leftover yarn or yarn in an unpopular color from round 7 up.*

Rnd 7 – 34: sc in all 14 st [14]
Stuff the leg firmly with fiberfill and continue stuffing as you go.
Rnd 35: (sc in next st, inc in next st) repeat 7 times [21]
Rnd 36: sc in next st, (inc in next st, sc in next 2 st) repeat 6 times, inc in next st, sc in next st [28]
Rnd 37: (sc in next 3 st, inc in next st) repeat 7 times [35]
Rnd 38: sc in all 35 st [35]
Fasten off and weave in the yarn end. Make sure the legs are stuffed very firmly and evenly. Set the legs aside and make the trouser legs.

TROUSER LEG

∗ *make 2, in graphite yarn*

Leave a long starting yarn tail. You're

going to need it to work another round around the bottom of the trouser leg later. Ch 24 and join with a slst to make a circle. Make sure the chain isn't twisted.
Rnd 1: sc in all 24 ch [24]
Rnd 2 – 6: sc in all 24 st [24]
Rnd 7: (sc in next 7 st, inc in next st) repeat 3 times [27]
Rnd 8 – 12: sc in all 27 st [27]
Rnd 13: sc in next 4 st, (inc in next st, sc in next 8 st) repeat 2 times, inc in next st, sc in next 4 st [30]
Rnd 14 – 18: sc in all 30 st [30]
Rnd 19: (sc in next 9 st, inc in next st) repeat 3 times [33]
Rnd 20 – 24: sc in all 33 st [33]
Rnd 25: inc in next st, sc in next 15 st, inc in next st, sc in next 16 st [35]
Rnd 26 – 30: sc in all 35 st [35]
Don't fasten off yet. Go back to round 1 and, using the yarn tail you left at the beginning, work slst around the bottom of the trouser leg. Fasten off and weave in the yarn end on the wrong side of your work.

Continue working on round 30. Crochet an additional 3-4 sc to move the beginning of the round to the side of the trouser leg and mark the last stitch you made, this is the new beginning of your round. Position the trouser leg over the leg and align the edges. In the next round, we'll join the leg and the trouser leg together.
Rnd 31: sc in all 35 st through both layers [35]
Fasten off, leaving a yarn tail. Join the second leg and trouser leg in the same way, but don't fasten off. In the next round, we'll join both trouser legs together and start crocheting the body.

BODY
✳ *continue in graphite yarn*

Rnd 1: join to the first trouser leg with a sc, sc in next 29 st on the first trouser leg, skip 5 st on the first trouser leg, skip 5 st on the second trouser leg, sc in the 6th st, sc in next 29 st on the second trouser leg [60]
Rnd 2: sc in all 60 st [60]
Rnd 3: (sc in next 9 st, inc in next st) repeat 6 times [66]
Use the yarn tail left on the first trouser leg to sew the gap between the legs closed.
Rnd 4: sc in next 5 st, (inc in next st, sc in next 10 st) repeat 5 times, inc in next st, sc in next 5 st [72]
Rnd 5: BLO sc in all 72 st [72]
Continue crocheting in a tapestry pattern, alternating graphite and mustard yellow yarn. Make sure that the dark sections on the jacket are centered and that the yellow sections are on the sides. Make a couple of additional stitches or undo a few if needed. The color change is indicated in italics before each part.
Rnd 6 – 19: *{mustard yellow}* sc in next 9 st, *{graphite}* sc in next 18 st, *{mustard yellow}* sc in next 18 st, *{graphite}* sc in next 18 st, *{mustard yellow}* sc in next 9 st [72] (picture 1)
Change to graphite yarn.
Rnd 20: sc in all 72 st [72]
Rnd 21: sc in next 5 st, (dec, sc in next 10 st) repeat 5 times, dec, sc in next 5 st [66]
Rnd 22: (sc in next 9 st, dec) repeat 6 times [60]
Change to mustard yellow yarn.
Rnd 23: sc in all 60 st [60]
Rnd 24: sc in next 9 st, (dec, sc in next 18 st) repeat

2 times, dec, sc in next 9 st [57]
Rnd 25: (sc in next 17 st, dec) repeat 3 times [54]
Rnd 26: sc in next 8 st, (dec, sc in next 16 st) repeat 2 times, dec, sc in next 8 st [51]
Rnd 27: (sc in next 15 st, dec) repeat 3 times [48]
Rnd 28: sc in next 7 st, (dec, sc in next 14 st) repeat 2 times, dec, sc in next 7 st [45]
Rnd 29: (sc in next 13 st, dec) repeat 3 times [42]
Slst in next st. Fasten off, leaving a long yarn tail. Make the sweater vest ribbing next (we find it easier to do while the doll is unstuffed). Hold the body with the legs pointing away from you and pull up a loop of graphite yarn in the last unworked front loop of round 4 of the body.
Ribbing: ch 2, FLO dc in all 72 st, slst in first st [72]
Fasten off and weave in the yarn end. Stuff the body very firmly with fiberfill.

HEAD
✳ *in nude yarn*

Rnd 1: start 6 sc in a magic ring [6]
Rnd 2: inc in all 6 st [12]
Rnd 3: (sc in next st, inc in next st) repeat 6 times [18]
Rnd 4: sc in next st, (inc in next st, sc in next 2 st) repeat 5 times, inc in next st, sc in next st [24]
Rnd 5: (sc in next 3 st, inc in next st) repeat 6 times [30]
Rnd 6: sc in next 2 st, (inc in next st, sc in next 4 st) repeat 5 times, inc in next st, sc in next 2 st [36]
Rnd 7: (sc in next 5 st, inc in next st) repeat 6 times [42]
Rnd 8: sc in next 3 st, (inc in next st, sc in next 6 st) repeat 5 times, inc in next st, sc in next 3 st [48]
Rnd 9: (sc in next 7 st, inc in next st) repeat 6 times [54]
Rnd 10: sc in next 4 st, (inc in next st, sc in next 8 st) repeat 5 times, inc in next st, sc in next 4 st [60]
Rnd 11: (sc in next 9 st, inc in next st) repeat 6 times [66]
Rnd 12 – 26: sc in all 66 st [66]
Rnd 27: (sc in next 9 st, dec) repeat 6 times [60]
Rnd 28: sc in next 4 st, (dec, sc in next 8 st) repeat 5 times, dec, sc in next 4 st [54]
Rnd 29: (sc in next 7 st, dec) repeat 6 times [48]
Stuff the head with fiberfill and continue stuffing as you go.
Rnd 30: sc in next 3 st, (dec, sc in next 6 st) repeat

5 times, dec, sc in next 3 st [42]
Rnd 31: BLO (sc in next 5 st, dec) repeat 6 times [36]
Rnd 32: sc in next 2 st, (dec, sc in next 4 st) repeat 5 times, dec, sc in next 2 st [30]
Rnd 33: (sc in next 3 st, dec) repeat 5 times [24]
Rnd 34: sc in next st, (dec, sc in next 2 st) repeat 5 times, dec, sc in next st [18]
Finish stuffing the head very firmly.
Rnd 35: (dec, sc in next st) repeat 6 times [12]
Rnd 36: dec 6 times [6]
Fasten off, leaving a yarn tail. Using a yarn needle, weave the yarn tail through the front loop of each remaining stitch and pull it tight to close. Weave in the yarn end. Sew the head and the body together using the leftover front loops of round 30 of the head. Stuff the neck area with more fiberfill before closing the seam (using a chopstick).

ARM
* make 2, start in nude yarn

Rnd 1: start 6 sc in a magic ring [6]
Rnd 2: (inc in next st, sc in next st) repeat 3 times [9]
Rnd 3: sc in all 9 st [9]
Rnd 4: sc in next 4 st, 5-dc-bobble in next st, sc in next 4 st [9]
Rnd 5 – 7: sc in all 9 st [9]
Change to mustard yellow yarn.
> **Note:** Make sure the color change is at the inside of the arm, add a few sc or undo a few to get to this point.

Rnd 8: FLO inc in all 9 st [18]
Rnd 9: sc in next st, (inc in next st, sc in next 2 st) repeat 5 times, inc in next st, sc in next st [24]
Rnd 10 – 11: sc in all 24 st [24]
Stuff the hand with fiberfill. Continue crocheting in a tapestry pattern, alternating mustard yellow and graphite yarn. Make sure that the thumb is in the middle of the dark section. Make a couple of additional stitches or undo a few if needed. The color change is indicated in italics before each part.
Rnd 12 – 28: {mustard yellow} sc in next 11 st, {graphite} sc in next 10 st, {mustard yellow} sc in next 3 st [24]
Continue in mustard yellow yarn.
Rnd 29: sc in next 3 st, (dec, sc in next 6 st) repeat 2 times, dec, sc in next 3 st [21]
Rnd 30: sc in all 21 st [21]
Rnd 31: (sc in next 5 st, dec) repeat 3 times [18]
Rnd 32: sc in all 18 st [18] (pictures 2-3)
Stuff the sleeve lightly with fiberfill, so the arms don't stick out too much after sewing. Make a couple of additional sc or undo a few to get to the opposite side of the thumb. Flatten the arm and work the next round through both layers to close.
Rnd 33: sc in all 9 st [9]
Fasten off, leaving a long tail for sewing. Sew the arms to the sides of the body, with the top edges of the dark sections on the sleeves on round 22 of the body (the last round crocheted in graphite). Make sure that the thumbs are facing inwards.

TROUSER POCKETS
* make 2, start in graphite yarn

Ch 7. Stitches are worked around both sides of the foundation chain.
Rnd 1: start in second ch from hook, sc in next 5 ch, 4 sc in next ch. Continue on the other side of the foundation chain, sc in next 4 ch, 3 sc in next ch [16]
Rnd 2 – 4: sc in all 16 st [16]
Change to mustard yellow yarn.
Rnd 5: BLO sc in all 16 st [16]
Rnd 6 – 10: sc in all 16 st [16]
Rnd 11: (dec, sc in next 6 st) repeat 2 times [14]
Fasten off, leaving a long yarn tail. Flatten your work and sew the gap at the (mustard yellow) bottom closed (picture 4). Sew the pockets to the outer sides of the trouser legs, at 3-4 rounds below the tips of the hands, so Stefan can easily access their contents (picture 5). Decorate each pocket with tiny buttons.

MULLET
✳ *in light brown yarn*

diagram 2 on page 135

Leave a long starting yarn tail. Ch 5. Crochet in rows.
Row 1: start in second ch from hook, sc in next 4 ch,
ch 1, (ch 16, start in third ch from hook, dc in next
12 ch, hdc in next ch, sc in next ch) repeat 16 times,
ch 6, start in second ch from hook, sc in next 4 ch.
Fasten off, leaving a long yarn tail.

> **Note:** *The mullet should look a bit like a garland (the
> shorter parts at the edges are Stefan's sideburns).*

Sew the top edge of the mullet to the back of the head,
between rounds 18 and 19, using both yarn tails. Using
a single strand of light brown yarn, secure the tresses
onto the head at 5-6 rounds below the top edge of the
mullet, so they don't curl up too much (picture 6). Make
sure to leave a little space between the smaller sideburns and the bigger curls, as the ears will be attached
between them.

HAIR PATCH
✳ *in light brown yarn*

Ch 14. Stitches are worked around both sides of the
foundation chain.
Rnd 1: start in third ch from hook, dc in next 11 ch,
6 dc in next ch. Continue on the other side of the foundation chain, dc in next 10 ch, 5 dc in next ch [32]
Fasten off and weave in the yarn end. Using a single

strand of light brown yarn, sew the hair patch to the
top of Stefan's head (picture 7).

EAR
✳ *make 2, in nude yarn*

Leave a long starting yarn tail.
Rnd 1: start 7 sc in a magic ring [7]
Pull the magic ring tightly closed and fasten off, leaving
a long tail for sewing. Sew the ears to both sides of the
head, right behind the sideburns. Weave in the yarn ends.

BASEBALL HAT

CAP
✳ *start in mustard yellow yarn*

Rnd 1: start 6 sc in a magic ring [6]
Rnd 2: sc in all 6 st [6]
Rnd 3: BLO inc in all 6 st [12]
Rnd 4: (sc in next st, inc in next st) repeat 6 times [18]
Rnd 5: sc in next st, (inc in next st, sc in next 2 st) repeat
5 times, inc in next st, sc in next st [24]
Rnd 6: (sc in next 3 st, inc in next st) repeat 6 times [30]
Rnd 7: sc in next 2 st, (inc in next st, sc in next 4 st)
repeat 5 times, inc in next st, sc in next 2 st [36]
Rnd 8: (sc in next 5 st, inc in next st) repeat 6 times [42]
Rnd 9: sc in next 3 st, (inc in next st, sc in next 6 st)
repeat 5 times, inc in next st, sc in next 3 st [48]

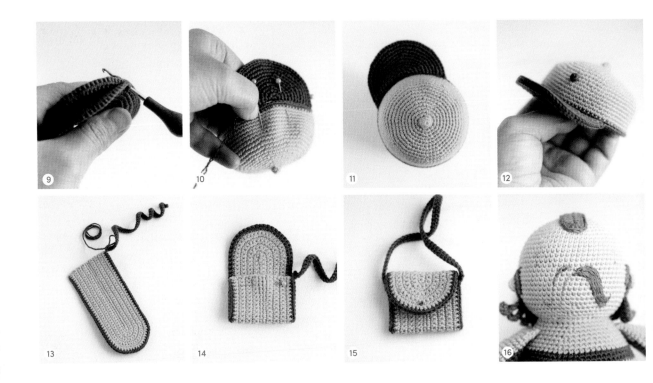

Rnd 10: (sc in next 7 st, inc in next st) repeat 6 times [54]
Rnd 11: sc in next 4 st, (inc in next st, sc in next 8 st) repeat 5 times, inc in next st, sc in next 4 st [60]
Rnd 12: (sc in next 9 st, inc in next st) repeat 6 times [66]
Rnd 13: sc in next 5 st, (inc in next st, sc in next 10 st) repeat 5 times, inc in next st, sc in next 5 st [72]
Rnd 14 – 21: sc in all 72 st [72]
Change to graphite yarn.
Rnd 22: sc in all 72 st [72] (picture 8)
Slst in next st. Fasten off and weave in the yarn end.

VISOR
* in graphite yarn

Rnd 1: start 8 sc in a magic ring [8]
Rnd 2: inc in all 8 st [16]
Rnd 3: (sc in next st, inc in next st) repeat 8 times [24]
Rnd 4: sc in next st, (inc in next st, sc in next 2 st) repeat 7 times, inc in next st, sc in next st [32]
Rnd 5: (sc in next 3 st, inc in next st) repeat 8 times [40]
Rnd 6: sc in next 2 st, (inc in next st, sc in next 4 st)

repeat 7 times, inc in next st, sc in next 2 st [48]
Rnd 7: (sc in next 5 st, inc in next st) repeat 8 times [56]
Rnd 8: sc in next 3 st, (inc in next st, sc in next 6 st) repeat 7 times, inc in next st, sc in next 3 st [64]
Rnd 9: (sc in next 7 st, inc in next st) repeat 8 times [72]
Rnd 10: sc in next 4 st, (inc in next st, sc in next 8 st) repeat 7 times, inc in next st, sc in next 4 st [80]
Rnd 11: (sc in next 9 st, inc in next st) repeat 8 times [88]
The visor doesn't need to be stuffed. Fold your work in half (with the wrong side on the inside). Work the next round through both layers to close.
Rnd 12: slst in all 44 st [44] (picture 9)
Fasten off and weave in the yarn end. Pin the visor to the edge of the cap and, using a single strand of graphite yarn, sew it neatly in place (pictures 10-11). Decorate the front of the hat with a small gray button (picture 12).

MAILBAG
* start in mustard yellow yarn

Ch 31. Stitches are worked around both sides of the

foundation chain.

Rnd 1: start in second ch from hook, sc in next 29 ch, 3 sc in next ch. Continue on the other side of the foundation chain, sc in next 29 ch, ch 1, turn [61]

Continue crocheting in rows.

Row 2: sc in next 29 st, inc in next 3 st, sc in next 29 st, ch 1, turn [64]

Row 3: sc in next 29 st, (sc in next st, inc in next st) repeat 3 times, sc in next 29 st, ch 1, turn [67]

Row 4: sc in next 30 st, (inc in next st, sc in next 2 st) repeat 2 times, inc in next st, sc in next 30 st, ch 1, turn [70]

Row 5: sc in next 29 st, (sc in next 3 st, inc in next st) repeat 3 times, sc in next 29 st, ch 1, turn [73]

Row 6: sc in next 31 st, (inc in next st, sc in next 4 st) repeat 2 times, inc in next st, sc in next 31 st, ch 1, turn [76]

Row 7: sc in next 29 st, (sc in next 5 st, inc in next st) repeat 3 times, sc in next 29 st, ch 1, turn [79]

Row 8: sc in next 32 st, (inc in next st, sc in next 6 st) repeat 2 times, inc in next st, sc in next 32 st, ch 1, turn [82]

Change to graphite yarn.

> **Note:** As the next row has no increases in it, make sure to work along the round part (the flap of the bag) loosely to keep it flat.

Row 9: sc in next 81 st, slst in next st [82]

Don't fasten off. Continue making the strap.

STRAP
※ *in graphite yarn*

Ch 71. Crochet in rows.

Row 1: start in second ch from hook, sc in all 70 ch [70]

Fasten off, leaving a yarn tail (picture 13). Fold the bottom part (about 10-12 stitches) up to form a pocket (picture 14). Using a single strand of graphite yarn, sew the sides of the bag closed. Sew the loose end of the strap in place too. Decorate the bag flap with a tiny button (picture 15).

FINISHING TOUCHES

• Embroider the facial features. A water-soluble marker or sewing pins may come in handy to mark out the position of the eyes, eyebrows and cheeks first. The eyes are embroidered using one or two strands of graphite yarn or black embroidery thread. Position the eyes at 1 round above the top edge of the mullet, with an interspace of approximately 15-16 stitches. Embroider the cheeks underneath the eyes using pink embroidery thread.

• The English moustache is Stefan's pride and joy, so you'll have to invest some time in making it. It's 18 stitches wide and 9 stitches high. It's also a little bit asymmetrical, with the right part being slightly bigger than the left part. Map it out with a water-soluble marker and then cover it with random short stitches using one or two strands of light brown yarn (picture 16). Embroider the mouth using graphite yarn or black embroidery thread. Embroider the cheeks underneath the eyes using pink embroidery thread.

• Put the mailbag over Stefan's shoulder and put the hat onto his head. Put a folded piece of paper into the bag to make Stefan look busy and to strengthen the bag a bit too.

HABIBA

As her name suggests, ('habiba' means 'the loved one' in Arabic), Mrs. Habiba is the kindest, most loving and nurturing teacher one can have. She lets the kids play with her cat Bubbles after school and she always gives a comforting hug to anyone who needs it.

SKILL LEVEL

* *

SIZE

9.5" / 23.5 cm tall when made with the indicated yarn.

MATERIALS

- Fingering weight yarn in:
  • lilac
  • nude
  • jeans blue
  • pink
  • brick brown
  • mustard yellow
  • gray
  • fuchsia (leftover)
  • light gray (leftover)
- 7 steel / 1.5 mm crochet hook
- Scraps of black and pink yarn or embroidery thread (for the embroidery)
- Sewing needle
- Yarn needle
- Pins
- Pliers
- 2 flat buttons (diameter 0.5" / 1.4 cm) to strengthen the feet
- 2 small beads
- Fabric glue
- 3" / 8 cm of florist wire to make the butterfly
- Approx. 8" / 20 cm of green crafting wire to make the glasses
- Stitch markers
- Fiberfill for stuffing

Scan or visit
www.amigurumi.com/3915
to share pictures and find inspiration.

LEG

* *make 2, start in lilac yarn*

> **Note:** *Habiba has fake trousers that are similar to Oma's trousers. We start by crocheting the legs and trouser legs separately. We continue by attaching the trouser legs directly to the legs, then join the trouser legs together to create the body.*

Rnd 1: start 6 sc in a magic ring [6]
Rnd 2: inc in all 6 st [12]
Rnd 3: (sc in next st, inc in next st) repeat 6 times [18]
Rnd 4: BLO sc in all 18 st [18]
Rnd 5: sc in all 18 st [18]

> **Note:** *Insert a flat button inside the foot at this point. It's important to keep the soles flat as we want them to have the same shape as cute little hooves.*

Rnd 6: (dec, sc in next st) repeat 6 times [12]

> **Note:** *As the trousers are long and are not coming off, you won't be able to see much of the legs, so it would be smart and eco-friendly to use leftover yarn or yarn in an unpopular color from round 8 up.*

Rnd 7 – 26: sc in all 12 st [12]
Stuff the leg firmly with fiberfill and continue stuffing as you go.
Rnd 27: (sc in next 3 st, inc in next st) repeat 3 times [15]
Rnd 28: sc in next 2 st, (inc in next st, sc in next 4 st) repeat 2 times, inc in next st, sc in next 2 st [18]
Rnd 29: (sc in next 5 st, inc in next st) repeat 3 times [21]
Rnd 30: sc in next 3 st, (inc in next st, sc in next 6 st) repeat 2 times, inc in next st, sc in next 3 st [24]
Rnd 31: (sc in next 7 st, inc in next st) repeat 3 times [27]
Rnd 32: sc in all 27 st [27]
Fasten off and weave in the yarn end. Make sure the leg is stuffed very firmly and evenly. Set the legs aside and make the trouser legs.

TROUSER LEG

* *make 2, in jeans blue yarn*

Leave a very long starting yarn tail. You're going to need it to work another round around the bottom of the trouser leg later. Ch 21 and join with a slst to make a circle.

Make sure the chain isn't twisted.

Rnd 1: sc in all 21 ch [21]

Rnd 2 – 7: sc in all 21 st [21]

Don't fasten off yet. Go back to round 1 and, using the tail you left at the beginning, work slst around the bottom of the trouser leg. Fasten off and weave in the yarn end on the wrong side of your work. Continue working on round 7.

Rnd 8: sc in next 3 st, (inc in next st, sc in next 6 st) repeat 2 times, inc in next st, sc in next 3 st [24]

Rnd 9 – 15: sc in all 24 st [24]

Rnd 16: (sc in next 7 st, inc in next st) repeat 3 times [27]

Rnd 17 – 24: sc in all 27 st [27]

Crochet an additional 5 sc to move the beginning of the round to the side of the leg and mark the last stitch you made, this is the new beginning of the round. Position the trouser leg over the leg and align the edges. In the next round, we'll join the leg and the trouser leg together.

Rnd 25: sc in all 27 st through both layers [27]

Fasten off and weave in the yarn end. Join the second leg and trouser leg in the same way, but don't fasten off. In the next round, we'll join both trouser legs together and start crocheting the body.

BODY

❋ continue in jeans blue yarn

Rnd 1: sc in a st on the first trouser leg to join, sc in next 26 st of the first trouser leg, sc in all 27 st of the second trouser leg [54]

Crochet an additional 14 sc to move the beginning of the round to the side of the body and mark the last stitch you made. This is the new beginning of the round.

Rnd 2 – 5: sc in all 54 st [54]

Change to pink yarn.

Rnd 6: sc in all 54 st [54]

Rnd 7: work this round in BLO, sc in next 4 st, (inc in next st, sc in next 8 st) repeat 5 times, inc in next st, sc in next 4 st [60]

Rnd 8: (sc in next 9 st, inc in next st) repeat 6 times [66]

Rnd 9: sc in next 5 st, (inc in next st, sc in next 10 st) repeat 5 times, inc in next st, sc in next 5 st [72]

Rnd 10 – 15: sc in all 72 st [72]

Rnd 16: sc in next 11 st, (dec, sc in next 22 st) repeat 2 times, dec, sc in next 11 st [69]

Rnd 17: sc in all 69 st [69]

Rnd 18: (sc in next 21 st, dec) repeat 3 times [66]

Rnd 19: sc in all 66 st [66]

Rnd 20: sc in next 10 st, (dec, sc in next 20 st) repeat 2 times, dec, sc in next 10 st [63]

Rnd 21: sc in all 63 st [63]

Rnd 22: (sc in next 19 st, dec) repeat 3 times [60]

Rnd 23: sc in all 60 st [60]

Rnd 24: sc in next 9 st, (dec, sc in next 18 st) repeat 2 times, dec, sc in next 9 st [57]

Rnd 25: sc in all 57 st [57]

Rnd 26: (sc in next 17 st, dec) repeat 3 times [54]

Rnd 27: (sc in next 7 st, dec) repeat 6 times [48]

Rnd 28: sc in next 7 st, (dec, sc in next 14 st) repeat 2 times, dec, sc in next 7 st [45]

Rnd 29: (sc in next 13 st, dec) repeat 3 times [42]

Rnd 30: sc in next 6 st, (dec, sc in next 12 st) repeat 2 times, dec, sc in next 6 st [39]

Rnd 31: (sc in next 11 st, dec) repeat 3 times [36]

Rnd 32: sc in all 36 st [36]

Crochet an additional 4-5 sc to move the beginning of the round to the side of the body and mark the last stitch you made. This is the new beginning of the round. Change to nude yarn.

Rnd 33 – 34: sc in all 36 st [36]

Fasten off, leaving a long tail for sewing. Stuff the body very firmly with fiberfill.

SWEATER RIBBING

❋ in pink yarn

Hold the doll with the legs pointing away from you and pull up a loop of pink yarn in the last leftover front loop of round 6 of the body.

Rnd 1: FLO sc in all 54 st [54]

Rnd 2 – 3: (FPdc in next st, BPdc in next st) repeat 27 times [54]

Fasten off and weave in the yarn end (picture 1).

HEAD

❋ in nude yarn

Rnd 1: start 6 sc in a magic ring [6]

Rnd 2: inc in all 6 st [12]

Rnd 3: (sc in next st, inc in next st) repeat 6 times [18]

Rnd 4: sc in next st, (inc in next st, sc in next 2 st) repeat 5 times, inc in next st, sc in next st [24]

Rnd 5: (sc in next 3 st, inc in next st) repeat 6 times [30]

Rnd 6: sc in next 2 st, (inc in next st, sc in next 4 st) repeat 5 times, inc in next st, sc in next 2 st [36]

Rnd 7: (sc in next 5 st, inc in next st) repeat 6 times [42]

Rnd 8: sc in next 3 st, (inc in next st, sc in next 6 st) repeat 5 times, inc in next st, sc in next 3 st [48]

Rnd 9: (sc in next 7 st, inc in next st) repeat 6 times [54]

Rnd 10: sc in next 4 st, (inc in next st, sc in next 8 st) repeat 5 times, inc in next st, sc in next 4 st [60]

Rnd 11 – 22: sc in all 60 st [60]

Rnd 23: sc in next 4 st, (dec, sc in next 8 st) repeat 5 times, dec, sc in next 4 st [54]

Rnd 24: (sc in next 7 st, dec) repeat 6 times [48]
Stuff the head with fiberfill and continue stuffing as you go.

Rnd 25: sc in next 3 st, (dec, sc in next 6 st) repeat 5 times, dec, sc in next 3 st [42]

Rnd 26: (sc in next 5 st, dec) repeat 6 times [36]

Rnd 27: work this round in BLO, sc in next 2 st, (dec, sc in next 4 st) repeat 5 times, dec, sc in next 2 st [30]

Rnd 28: (sc in next 3 st, dec) repeat 6 times [24]

Rnd 29: sc in next st, (dec, sc in next 2 st) repeat 5 times, dec, sc in next st [18]
Finish stuffing the head very firmly.

Rnd 30: (dec, sc in next st) repeat 6 times [12]

Rnd 31: dec 6 times [6]
Fasten off, leaving a yarn tail. Using a yarn needle, weave the yarn tail through the front loop of each remaining stitch and pull it tight to close. Weave in the yarn end. Sew the head and the body together using the leftover front loops of round 26 of the head. Stuff the neck area firmly with more fiberfill before closing the seam (using a chopstick), but make sure the neck is prominent enough for the hijab Habiba will wear later.

ARM

* make 2, start in nude yarn

Rnd 1: start 6 sc in a magic ring [6]

Rnd 2: (sc in next st, inc in next st) repeat 3 times [9]

Rnd 3: sc in all 9 st [9]

Rnd 4: sc in next 4 st, 5-dc-bobble in next st, sc in next 4 st [9]

Rnd 5 – 7: sc in all 9 st [9]
Change to pink yarn.

> **Note:** Make sure the color change is at the inside of the arm, add a few sc or undo a few to get to this point.

Rnd 8: BLO sc in all 9 st [9]
Stuff the hand (the nude part) firmly with fiberfill.

Rnd 9: spike st in all 9 st [9]

Rnd 10: BLO inc in all 9 st [18]

Rnd 11: sc in next st, (inc in next st, sc in next 2 st) repeat 5 times, inc in next st, sc in next st [24]

Rnd 12 – 16: sc in all 24 st [24]
Rnd 17: sc in next 3 st, (dec, sc in next 6 st) repeat 2 times, dec, sc in next 3 st [21]
Rnd 18 – 20: sc in all 21 st [21]
Rnd 21: (sc in next 5 st, dec) repeat 3 times [18]
Rnd 22 – 24: sc in all 18 st [18]
Rnd 25: sc in next 2 st, (dec, sc in next 4 st) repeat 2 times, dec, sc in next 2 st [15]
Rnd 26 – 28: sc in all 15 st [15]
Stuff the sleeve only lightly with fiberfill, so the arms don't stick out too much after sewing.

Rnd 29: (sc in next 3 st, dec) repeat 3 times [12]
Rnd 30 – 31: sc in all 12 st [12]
Make a couple of additional sc or undo a few to get to the opposite side of the thumb. Flatten the arm and work the next round through both layers to close.
Rnd 32: sc in all 6 st [6]
Fasten off, leaving a yarn tail for sewing. Sew the arms to the sides of the body, at 4-5 rounds below the neckline, between rounds 27-28.

HAIR

✳ *in brick brown yarn*

Rnd 1: start 6 sc in a magic ring [6]
Rnd 2: inc in all 6 st [12]
Rnd 3: (sc in next st, inc in next st) repeat 6 times [18]
Rnd 4: sc in next st, (inc in next st, sc in next 2 st) repeat 5 times, inc in next st, sc in next st [24]
Rnd 5: (sc in next 3 st, inc in next st) repeat 6 times [30]
Rnd 6: sc in next 2 st, (inc in next st, sc in next 4 st) repeat 5 times, inc in next st, sc in next 2 st [36]
Rnd 7: (sc in next 5 st, inc in next st) repeat 6 times [42]
Rnd 8: sc in next 3 st, (inc in next st, sc in next 6 st) repeat 5 times, inc in next st, sc in next 3 st [48]
Rnd 9: (sc in next 7 st, inc in next st) repeat 6 times [54]

> **Note:** *if you're not planning to take Habiba's hijab off, you can fasten off here and sew this piece to the head (as you can only see a part of it from under the headpiece). If you want to give your doll options, continue crocheting the hair strands.*

Ch 13. Continue crocheting in rows.
Row 1: start in second ch from hook, sc in next ch, hdc in next 6 ch, sc in next 5 ch, sc in next 2 st, turn [14]
Row 2: skip 2 st, BLO sc in next 5 st, BLO hdc in next 6 st, sc in next st, ch 1, turn [12] (pictures 2-3)
Row 3: sc in next st, BLO hdc in next 6 st, BLO sc in next 5 st, sc in next 2 st, turn [14]
Row 4 – 31: repeat Row 2 and 3 alternately (picture 4).
Row 32: repeat Row 2 [12]
Row 33: sc in next st, BLO hdc in next 6 st, BLO sc in next 5 st, slst in next st [13]
Continue making a single strand of hair for Habiba's fringe. Ch 20.
Row 34: start in second ch from hook, slst in next 2 ch, sc in next 15 ch, slst in next 2 ch. Fasten off (picture 5).

> **Note:** *The hair should look like a chocolate tartlet someone has already had a bite of. Wait to sew on the hair until the hijab is finished.*

HIJAB

As crocheted fabric is quite thick and stiff to fold, we've decided to cheat a little bit and not make a traditional shawl. Habiba's hijab is actually a bonnet with a long scarf attached to the bottom edge.

BONNET

✳ *in mustard yellow yarn*

Ch 8. Crochet in rows.
Row 1: start in second ch from hook, hdc in next 6 ch, 6 hdc in next ch. Continue on the other side of the foundation chain, hdc in next 6 ch, ch 1, turn [18]
Row 2: hdc in next 6 st, hdc inc in next 6 st, hdc in next 6 st, ch 1, turn [24]
Row 3: hdc in next 6 st, (hdc in next st, hdc inc in next st) repeat 6 times, hdc in next 6 st, ch 1, turn [30]
Row 4: hdc in next 7 st, (hdc inc in next st, hdc in next 2 st) repeat 5 times, hdc inc in next st, hdc in next 7 st, ch 1, turn [36]
Row 5: hdc in next 6 st, (hdc in next 3 st, hdc inc in next st) repeat 6 times, hdc in next 6 st, ch 1, turn [42]
Row 6: hdc in next 8 st, (hdc inc in next st, hdc in next 4 st) repeat 5 times, hdc inc in next st, hdc in next 8 st [48] (picture 6)
Row 7 – 14: hdc in all 48 st, ch 1, turn [48]
Row 15: hdc in next 7 st, (hdc2tog, hdc in next 14 st) repeat 2 times, hdc2tog, hdc in next 7 st, ch 1, turn [45]
Row 16: sc in all 45 st [45] (picture 7)
Don't fasten off yet. Continue making the scarf at the bottom.

SCARF

✳ *continue in mustard yellow yarn*

Ch 73. Continue crocheting in rows.
Row 1: start in second ch from hook, hdc in all 72 ch, work hdc along the row-ends of the bonnet (we ended up with 34 hdc, but if you have another number of stitches, it's ok too: just don't forget to count them so the number of stitches in the next rounds are even), ch 90, ch 1, turn [196] (picture 8)
Row 2: hdc in next 90 ch, hdc in next 106 st, ch 1, turn [196]
Row 3 – 5: hdc in all 196 st, ch 1, turn [196]
Row 6: hdc in next 90 st, sc in next 2 st, slst in next st [93]
Leave the remaining stitches unworked.

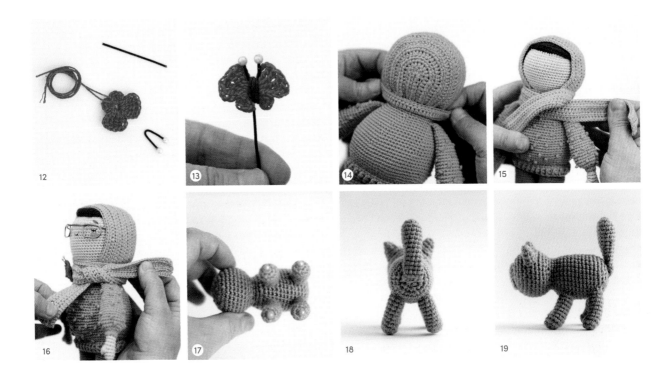

Fasten off and weave in the yarn end (picture 9).
Try on the hair and the hijab and undo a couple of rows on the hair if needed. We want only a little bit of the fringe to show. Pin the hair into place and sew it to the head with a single strand of brick brown yarn. Sew the end of the fringe to the opposite side of the face (picture 10) and decorate it with a couple of stitches in a contrasting color to mimic hairpins (picture 11).

BUTTERFLY BROOCH
∗ in fuchsia yarn

Diagram 10 on page 135

Rnd 1: start ch 2, 2 dc, ch 2, slst, (ch 4, 4 dtr, ch 4, slst) repeat 2 times, ch 2, 2 dc, ch 2, slst in a magic ring. Pull the magic ring tightly closed. Fasten off, leaving a long yarn tail.

> **Note:** If you're using a soft yarn, you may need to starch your work before moving to the next steps, as the wings are likely to curl up.

Cut two pieces of thin crafting wire (about 1.5" / 4 cm long). One of them will be the pin (you can use an actual sewing pin instead as well) and the second will be used to make the butterfly's antennae.
Bend one of the pieces to form a "V" shape and glue a small bead on each end. Use a piece of leftover yarn in a contrasting color and secure the antennae on the butterfly by wrapping the yarn over it and around the center of the piece a few times. Tie a knot and weave in the yarn ends. Secure the finished butterfly on top of the second piece of wire (pictures 12-13).

FINISHING TOUCHES

• Cover (at least) the front of Habiba's sweater with random French knots, skipping the areas underneath the arms (because you don't want the arms to stick out like a scarecrow).

• Embroider the facial features. A water-soluble marker or sewing pins may come in handy to mark out the position of the eyes, eyebrows, mouth and cheeks first. The eyes are embroidered using one or two strands of graphite yarn or black embroidery thread. Position the eyes 5 rounds below the fringe, with an interspace of approximately 12 stitches. Embroider the mouth 1 round below the eyes, centered between the eyes. Embroider the eyebrows using one or two strands of brick brown yarn. Embroider the cheeks underneath the eyes using pink embroidery thread.

- Put the hijab on and fold the center back part of the scarf up, so it hugs the neck nicely (picture 14). Wrap the ends around Habiba's neck and tie a knot if desired. If you're not going to take it off, you can sew it on with a couple of stitches (pictures 15-16).
- Make the glasses out of a piece of crafting wire the same way you made Opa's glasses (instructions on p. 51).
- Pin the butterfly brooch in place.

BUBBLES THE CAT

Bubbles is always eating Mrs. Habiba's sushi dinner and acting very innocent about it. She loves to cuddle and often watches the cartoon show Tom and Jerry while Mrs. Habiba is working at school.

> *Note: As the body parts of the cat are all very small, we recommend not to use the whole yarn tail for sewing, but to split it into strands instead.*

HEAD AND BODY

✻ in gray yarn

Rnd 1: start 6 sc in a magic ring [6]
Rnd 2: inc in all 6 st [12]
Rnd 3: (sc in next st, inc in next st) repeat 6 times [18]
Rnd 4: sc in next st, (inc in next st, sc in next 2 st) repeat 5 times, inc in next st, sc in next st [24]
Rnd 5: (sc in next 3 st, inc in next st) repeat 6 times [30]
Rnd 6 – 11: sc in all 30 st [30]
Rnd 12: (sc in next 3 st, dec) repeat 6 times [24]
Rnd 13: sc in next st, (dec, sc in next 2 st) repeat 5 times, dec, sc in next st [18]
Stuff the head firmly with fiberfill.
Rnd 14: sc in next 12 st, (inc in next st, sc in next st) repeat 3 times [21]
Rnd 15: sc in next 13 st, (inc in next st, sc in next 2 st)

repeat 2 times, inc in next st, sc in next st [24]
Rnd 16: sc in next 12 st, (inc in next st, sc in next 3 st) repeat 3 times [27]
Rnd 17 – 26: sc in all 27 st [27]
Rnd 27: (sc in next 7 st, dec) repeat 3 times [24]
Rnd 28: sc in next st, (dec, sc in next 2 st) repeat 5 times, dec, sc in next st [18]
Rnd 29: (sc in next st, dec) repeat 6 times [12]
Stuff the body firmly with fiberfill.
Rnd 30: dec 6 times [6]
Fasten off, leaving a yarn tail. Using a yarn needle, weave the yarn tail through the front loop of each remaining stitch and pull it tight to close. Weave in the yarn end.

LEG
* make 4, in gray yarn

Rnd 1: start 6 sc in a magic ring [6]
Rnd 2: inc in all 6 st [12]
Rnd 3: sc in all 12 st [12]
Rnd 4: dec 3 times, sc in next 6 st [9]
Rnd 5 – 10: sc in all 9 st [9]
Fasten off, leaving a yarn tail. Stuff the legs firmly so the cat can stand without support. Pin the legs to the belly (the more rounded part of the body), between rounds 18 and 26, with an interspace of 4-5 stitches (picture 17). Make sure your construction is stable and your cat is not rolling to one side. Sew the legs in place.

EAR
* make 2, in gray yarn

Rnd 1: start 4 sc in a magic ring [4]
Rnd 2: (inc in next st, sc in next st) repeat 2 times [6]
Rnd 3: (inc in next st, sc in next st) repeat 3 times [9]
Rnd 4: sc in next st, (inc in next st, sc in next 2 st) repeat 2 times, inc in next st, sc in next st [12]
Fasten off, leaving a yarn tail. Sew the ears on top of

the head, with an interspace of 5-6 stitches.

MUZZLE
* in light gray yarn

Ch 6. Crochet around both sides of the foundation chain.
Rnd 1: start in second ch from hook, inc in this ch, sc in next 3 ch, 4 sc in next ch. Continue on the other side of the foundation chain, sc in next 3 ch, inc in next ch [14] Fasten off and weave in the yarn end. Sew the muzzle in the center of the face. Embroider the eyes and nose with leftover yarn from making Habiba's wardrobe.

TAIL
* in gray yarn

Rnd 1: start 6 sc in a magic ring [6]
Rnd 2: inc in all 6 st [12]
Rnd 3 – 7: sc in all 12 st [12]
Rnd 8: (dec, sc in next 4 st) repeat 2 times [10]
Rnd 9 – 14: sc in all 10 st [10]
Stuff the tail with fiberfill, but don't stuff the last 4-5 rounds. Flatten the tail and work the next round through both layers to close.
Rnd 15: sc in all 5 st [5]
Fasten off, leaving a yarn tail. Sew the tail to the back of the cat's body, pointing upwards (pictures 18-19).

BOW
* in pink yarn

Leave a long starting yarn tail.
Row 1: (ch 12, join with a slst, sc in all 12 ch) repeat 2 times, (ch 6, start in second ch from hook, sc in this ch, sc in next 4 ch, slst in next ch) repeat 2 times.
Fasten off, leaving a long yarn tail. Wrap the yarn tails a couple of times around the middle of the bow and tie a knot. Use these yarn tails to secure the bow on the cat's neck. Hide one yarn end inside the body, the second one will be the leash. Tie the cat's leash to Habiba's wrist.

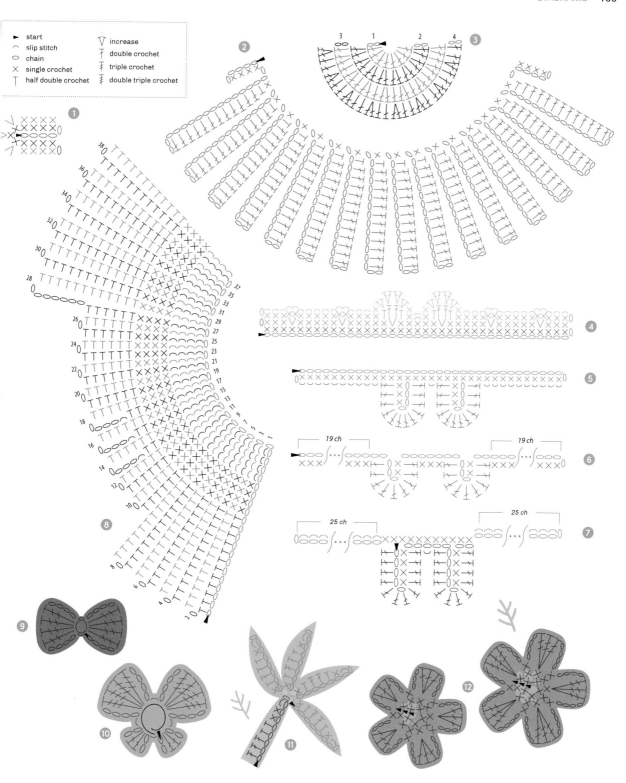

start
slip stitch
chain
single crochet
half double crochet
increase
double crochet
triple crochet
double triple crochet

Thank you from Granny's Crochet Hook (Dasha and Kate)

We'd really like to express our sincere gratitude to our lovely editors Joke and Dora for bringing this book idea to life and for being very patient and tolerating of all our if's, but's and we-don't-know's. ✶ A huge thank you to all the testers who worked hard and were really kind: Ashton Kirkham, Jill Constantine, Kristi Randmaa, Serena Chew, Iris Dongo, Barbara Roman, Annegret Siegert, Shannon Kishbaugh, Chrissy Rivers, Luisa Willem, Marianne Rosqvist, Amy Jones, Bianka Karolkiewicz, Lutgarde van Dijck, Marjan Peustjens, Ilonka Ladenius, Christina Marie, Caroline Vandier, Anna Persson, Karen Celestine Lee, Karina Green, Sonia Fox, Josephine Laurin, Julita Zacharz, Adrienn Weber, Silke Bridgman, Sabina Escrig, Jimena Bouso, Ida Stup, Sandra Zheng, Louisa Wong, Dóra Sipos-Járási and Sandra Belleval ✶ A special thank you to our local coffee shop owner Vova Shestakov for getting us fueled with caffeine and helping us with photographs when we needed an extra pair of hands. ✶ To Lydia Tresselt and Yan Schenkel for being very inspiring, constantly laughing at our silly makes and encouraging us. ✶ To our instafriends Natasha Tishchenko and June Mira for always being willing to help and actually helping us A LOT. ✶ To Agnes Sanches and Ioanna Papadopoulou for their infectious resilience and good vibes they're always able to project onto others. ✶ To Nour Abdallah for creating all these funny characters and allowing us to turn them into crocheted dolls. ✶ To all the beautiful people who support us by liking, sharing and commenting on our posts, buying patterns and making us want to continue. ✶ And to you!

Thank you from Nour

I would like to thank both Kate and Dasha for perfectly transforming my vision into crochet dolls, without them this book wouldn't have existed. ✶ Thank you to everyone who helped and supported us on every single step of the way. Thanks to you, we made it this far.